Over the Rainbow
India's Queer Heroes

Aditya Tiwari

juggernaut

JUGGERNAUT BOOKS
C-I-128, First Floor, Sangam Vihar, Near Holi Chowk,
New Delhi 110080, India

First published by Juggernaut Books 2023

10 9 8 7 6 5 4 3 2 1

P-ISBN: 9789353451752
E-ISBN: 9789353451769

Trigger warning: Some chapters in this book discuss emotional
abuse from family members upon identifying as a member of the
LGBTQ+ community – this may be difficult for some readers. They
also contain information about violence; discrimination on the basis
of caste, class, sexuality; gender dysphoria; and the complexity of
LGBTQ+ lives. Please engage in self-care as you read this book.

Typeset in Adobe Caslon Pro by R. Ajith Kumar, Noida

Printed at Manipal Technologies Limited, Manipal

Contents

Contents

Preface

I grew up gay in Jabalpur, a small city in Madhya Pradesh. In Jabalpur, you couldn't be openly gay. So, as a teenager, there weren't enough people around me in whose shade I could take shelter – we all need people to look up to, after all, whether we are young or old, male or female, binary or transgender, straight, bisexual or gay. As a child, I was told I was a lot of things and 'successful' wasn't one of them! Nor were there voices like mine being represented in mainstream media. There are many like me in India and around the world, and we all feel like we never belonged anywhere . . .

I longed to see someone from a smaller city like mine show up in the mainstream, someone who could represent me. This is what led me to become a writer, publishing my first book of poems and now this anthology. In it I have told the stories of nineteen trailblazers of our country's

LGBTQ+ movement, many of whom are well known, but many who might be new to you. Some come from the poorest villages, others from prosperous upper-middle-class families. Some have had an education, and many have had to drop out of school due to the pressures they have faced. Some are gay, some transgender. But they all have one thing in common. The battles they faced and won both socially and humanly are immense. Their courage is extraordinary. Each has made India an easier and a better place for the next generation of the LGBTQ+ community.

The history of India's LGBTQ+ movement isn't synonymous with the one in the West. While we must never forget trailblazers like Marsha P. Johnson or Sylvia Rivera during Pride month, in India we must also acknowledge the ferocity of those numerous hijras and kothis who have been at the forefront of the movement for centuries. It is also important to mention the intersectionality of caste and class, which made all our heroes' journeys even more challenging. The Pride flag alone is insufficient to make one whole sari for a hijra who has to clap and strip naked on the streets to protect herself. In this book, I have tried to create a list that reflects these complexities.

The idea of 'icons' through a queer lens will never be

complete; we are all heroes, trendsetters and inspirations in our lives, in our own ways. Coming down to just nineteen names was the most difficult part of this project. Even then, I have missed out on countless names of LGBTQ+ individuals and collectives who continue to resist the cis-temic oppression, especially the ones who have been visible and not seen by society and media, and for that, I would like to apologize to the community at large.

To my fellow queer friends, I hope that when you hold this book in your hands, you cherish the lives of these people and also think of those countless voices who will never be seen or heard but will continue to live and leave behind their impact, even if it may not be felt widely . . . To our heterosexual counterparts, when you hold this book in your hands, ask yourself if you've made even a slight difference in making this world a bit more loving. If you don't have an answer, reassess why, and that is the day when the real work begins.

Today, as I sit down to put this book together with a strong sense of freedom and pride, it is because of the lives of various others before me. They have opened colossal doors for people like me in Jabalpur, Raipur, Rampur or Bilaspur that didn't exist many years ago. At a time like this, when we are amid a monumental hearing on marriage equality in India, whatever the judgment might be, I believe it is a moment to celebrate our journey.

Aditya Tiwari
28 April 2023

Pawan Dhall, Owais Khan and Rafique-Ul-Haque-Dowjah-Ranjan

The Friendship Walk '99

It was a modest, nearly invisible, march. On 2 July 1999, a mere fifteen participants, wearing identical yellow T-shirts with a caption reading 'Walk on the Rainbow' showed up to walk for queer rights in Kolkata. From this small beginning developed the successful Pride marches, which seek to create a community and honour the history of the LGBTQ+ movement of India. Today, Pride marches in the country have expanded dramatically with a thousand to three thousand people participating across more than twenty cities.

But things were very different twenty years ago. The world may have been about to enter a shiny, new millennium but India was still stuck in the past when it came to LGBTQ+ rights. Owais Khan did not feel seen. While queers around the world were marching after the 1969 Stonewall riots in New York, organized against the police raid and the harassment faced by the queer community in their everyday lives, India sorely missed queer visibility.

Owais, heavily influenced by Gandhi, just wanted a padayatra, a walk, to try and build a bridge between the queer community and other sections of society. On 28 April 1999, he posted his idea of a Pride padayatra to the LGBT India group on Yahoo. The post was full of anguish and a strong desire to bring Indian queers out of the shadow. Owais wrote, 'We are still as invisible as we were 52 years ago.'[1] While thousands in New York were celebrating 'Gay Liberation Day', he asked 'Can we not do a small pada-yatra complete with pink triangles and rainbow-coloured peacocks? Perhaps not a Pride Parade if a lot of us do not want to be seen thus? Perhaps just a celebration of Liberty Day?'[2]

It was a revolutionary idea, and as it always happens with new ideas, it was met with resistance. Pawan Dhall, a long-time queer organizer in Kolkata and one of the original fifteen, started out feeling unsure about the idea. He said, 'Initially I had my reservations because I am a person who doesn't like stalling the traffic . . . My point was that if you are doing something in Calcutta, do something new and it should not be just another procession.'[3] But Owais had made up his mind, the walk was happening, even if he had to do it alone. Ultimately his sheer determination helped achieve the final consensus among the other organizers, the other two leaders being Pawan Dhall and Rafique-Ul-Haque-Dowjah-Ranjan.

In India in 1999, unlike today, there wasn't a diverse range of queer voices sufficiently audible for anyone to pay attention to them. There were no drag queens at the front, no vehicles, floats or loudspeakers, and no slogans that shouted 'Aadmi Hoon Aadmi Se Pyaar Karta Hoon' (I am a man who is in love with a man).

Technology wasn't as advanced as it is today. There were no dating apps like we have today and gay men would often meet up or converse using MSM (men who have sex with men)[4] sites or Yahoo. Later, many even in small towns would go to cybercafes to access sites like PlanetRomeo, which was started in 2002. But that was still three years away.

LGBT India started planning Friendship Walk in many locations via Yahoo groups and listservs. But first they had to come up with a name. The group initially thought of calling it the Humans Rights March, but that seemed too vague. Their imagination was running wild trying to figure a name for the event, anything but gay-adjacent names were acceptable. Eventually, they hit on 'Friendship Walk'. It was open to interpretation in all the right ways; it also sounded innocent and welcoming.

Kolkata came up as a natural choice to hold the walk. Mumbai had visibility, with queer issues already at the fore, thanks to Humsafar Trust and other organizations. But given the strong presence of Shiv Sena and the BJP, there could be political tensions with the Hindu extremists terming such a walk as 'anti-Indian' and 'foreign invasion'. 'Calcutta had activism and Owais felt that Calcutta has always been a hotbed of revolution,' Pawan would later say.[5] Owais too believed that Kolkata was special. 'I believed and still believe that Calcuttans have a much longer view than others. Calcuttans are willing to listen, and give more space to others. A lot of things started in Calcutta ... The culture of Calcutta permits you to say things that even they might not like to listen to. I was very close to Calcutta, Pawan and Ranjan.'[6]

Kolkata was not just an important base of LGBT India but was also the safest place for the first march. In 1996, when *Fire*, a film about lesbian sexuality was released, angry protests broke out in different parts of India. But for some reason, Kolkata seemed to be the only calm place amid all the outrage.

What was expected to be an event of thirty people ended up with just half the attendance. Fifteen was not a big number and a march with this strength was not even considered successful, but it was not about success, it wasn't even a fight, nobody was winning; it was just the gays trying to make the queer community as a whole visible.

Ashok Row Kavi and Nitin Karani – prominent gay rights activists at that time – were just a few of the well-known names that were part of the walk that had participants from Kolkata, Mumbai and Bangalore. Then there were people like Navarun Gupta, who had quit his teaching job in Atlanta to be with his mother following his father's death in 1999, who joined the walk. 'It was exciting to learn about it. I wanted to go to Kolkata to visit my relatives so this was a good chance to kill two birds with one stone ... My relatives had no idea where I disappeared on the day of the walk,'[7] he recalled.

The tiny party was divided into two, with one group heading north of Kolkata and the other south. As they walked, the fifteen members talked to as many of the bystanders on the roads that they came across, explaining why they were marching. 'It was very important that we took everyone together, including those people who would feel that loving people of the same sex is wrong ...

If you are still nice to him, he would be nice to you. I did not want the foundation to be anything other than cooperative, loving and happy,'[8] said Owais Khan.

The teams visited several NGOs on the way, including WB SACS, Human Rights Organization and other organizations working to prevent AIDS. They met some well-known people, including Maitree Chatterjee, who was at that time one of the leading voices in the women's rights movement in Kolkata. The junior officer who met them from the Human Rights Organization was taken aback by the activists. 'He was completely surprised about what this issue was. What is lesbian, what is gay, what is bisexual,'[9] he asked them. The project director at WB SACS, too, remained ambivalent about his assistance, although he acknowledged that the problem required rapid attention from the perspective of HIV prevention.

But the response the fifteen men received from the general public, who patiently listened to them and respected the effort, was what surprised them the most. Many were astounded that such a law even existed! When Ashok Row Kavi, the founder of *Bombay Dost* and The Humsafar Trust (see Ashok Row Kavi), was asked by an old woman what they were protesting about, he told her that they were homosexuals and that the government forbade them from having relationships. 'Kheye dey kaaj nei (No one has any work), people are just policing private lives',[10] she replied. Another woman exclaimed asking whether the government's only responsibility was to observe what citizens did in their bedrooms.

By the time the two parties arrived at George Bhavan, Moulali, in Central Kolkata, where the walk culminated, the press had learnt of the event and inundated the location with reporters. The reporters complained they had not been invited to the walk and they had no pictures. So what appeared in the newspapers was a mock walk, that the activists did again in front of George Bhavan.

As a result of widespread news coverage, not just domestically but also from neighbouring countries like Pakistan and Bangladesh, there was soon a flood of attention on the initiative. 'It wasn't as if everybody was supportive, but it led to a lot of dialogue,'[11] said Pawan Dhall.

Some questioned the walk saying '. . . we were duplicating a Western concept and that it was too far ahead of its time,'[12] Rafique-Ul-Haque-Dowjah-Ranjan, a consultant in social research and communication at the time, recalled. Some MSM community members said that he was an attention-seeker and had chosen to wear a GAY label on his back to become popular.

For many of the marchers, the walk was not merely a political gesture but a personal coming out to the world. Rafique-Ul, who was well known in Kolkata for his art and activism, was still not out until this point. Coming out is nothing like metamorphosing into a butterfly, but it is regarded as one. Nothing changes physically, but the perspective of how one is seen completely shifts.

Something just like this happened with Rafique-Ul. His long-standing relationship with his didi, his immediate neighbour who taught him art, ended. Years later, she knocked on his door and said, 'Babu, I am sorry.'[13] He says the lesson he learnt was: 'If you know you are doing the right thing keep doing it. People will come around if not today, then in twenty years.'[14]

Even though there were fallouts and criticisms, there was also support. When they crossed paths outside a nearby bank, a grocery store owner Pawan had known for years approached him and said the work he was doing was very good. 'At a micro-level, change is happening, I realized,'[15] Pavan remarked.

None of the walkers in 1999 ever remotely suspected they were making history or that their actions would have a lasting impact on people's lives. Pawan acknowledged that there was a lot of progress, and the number of people involved and the enthusiasm levels had multiplied enormously.

Over the years, noticing there were enough people to take the movement forward, Owais decided to take the backseat. 'I don't feel so much of a need to be very active in the activist part. I got my inspiration from Mahatma Gandhi, and he is a very important entity in my life. He fought as long as he thought he should and once he saw others would take forward, he left. That thought process has got internalized in me. There are enough people now.'[16] He still has his yellow T-shirt though.

Now that India had enough faces to take the queer movement forward, Pawan also raised concerns regarding the commercialization of what they once started in India. He felt that while there was a move towards greater inclusion of people and issues in the Pride Walks, there was also a trend towards making it a spectacle rather than a platform for protest. 'I hope there is less loud music and less balloons and more shouting slogans,' he said.[17]

After 1999, the walk didn't resume until four years later, in June 2003, thanks to Rafique-Ul-Haque-Dowjah-Ranjan, who revived the idea once more. About fifty people participated in the walk this time, which began at Park Circus Maidan and ended at the Jagadbandhu

Institution. Over two hundred people joined the march the following year – a four-fold increase. Cities like Mumbai, Bangalore and Bhubaneswar joined the trend after Kolkata's Pride Walks and had their first Pride events in the 2000s.

The Friendship Walk of 1999 is a reminder in history that the LGBTQ+ visibility movement in India, just like any other movement for a progressive society, started with a smattering number of people. It eventually became an event observed annually in different parts of India, bringing together the Indian queer community. The essence of inclusivity that we see today in the Indian demographic scene started with just fifteen gays and now it has pulsated into a platform for queer voices across the country. Next time whenever you see a Pride Walk in India, do not hesitate, just tag along for another walk of friendship.

Anjali Gopalan

The Pioneer

Anjali Gopalan, founder of the Naz Foundation (India) Trust, has been one of the most vocal champions of the LGBTQ+ community in India. She has been at the forefront of the movement, even at a time when the discussion regarding HIV/AIDS was stigmatized. Anjali has moved the courts of India in some of the country's most monumental moments that make India's queer history.

Born in 1957 in Chennai, Tamil Nadu, Anjali was raised in a family that instilled in her a sense of service and a belief in the power of standing up for what is right. When she went to the US for higher studies, she began working with undocumented migrant workers from Haiti and Latin America. It was her first exposure to

HIV, a new disease at that time. From close quarters, she saw how the affected grappled with its existence. 'HIV changes you as a person – how you think and respond. You question yourself, your culture and your morality.'[1] Working with them, she also discovered her passion lay in activism.

When the thirty-year-old Anjali returned to India in the late 1980s, India was becoming globalized but wealth inequality, class division and casteism persisted. HIV existed only in the shadows.

It was slowly affecting a number of different communities in ways that were very different from the US – there were the female sex workers and the migrant and trucker communities that they largely serviced, the injecting drug users (IDUs) and then there was a category known as MSM (men who have sex with men)[2] as well as transgenders. Each of these communities were also poor and disenfranchized without access to information, awareness or health care.

In Delhi, while setting up the first HIV clinic in 1994, Anjali began working with orphans with HIV – these were the children of young mothers who had been claimed by the disease. But as she became more involved, she found herself called to advocate for another group who needed her voice – young gay men whose families had disowned them.

Author Suketu Mehta, who met Anjali in 1995 when she had just started out, wrote, 'At the time, doctors and nurses in some Delhi hospitals would not touch people infected with HIV. Anjali not only touched them; she took them into her home and danced with them. She escorted me to the hidden places where gays and lesbians met: in Nehru Park on Sunday evenings and at a party where men arrived garbed as Bollywood heroines from the 1950s and 60s'.[3] Soon Anjali was not only assisting gay men but also their families who came to her asking for medicines to treat their child or kin so that they could be cured of the way they felt. 'It's when I really started to see the cultural paradigm shift that needed to happen in our society,' she said.[4]

Over the years, the Naz Foundation (India) Trust she founded has done more than any other organization to advance the rights of gays and transgenders in India. This groundbreaking organization has relentlessly focused on the fight against HIV/AIDS, with a particular emphasis on the empowerment of women, children and the LGBTQ+ community.

Under Anjali's visionary leadership, the Naz Foundation set up the country's first holistic home for vulnerable HIV-positive children in 2001. Recognizing the urgent need for comprehensive care, she not only provided shelter but also trained health professionals and caregivers to ensure the well-being of those affected by the disease. Her pioneering efforts expanded the scope of the existing facilities, enabling infected children to receive multifaceted care within nurturing homes and foster care environments.

The same year, the foundation, with support from The Lawyers Collective and under the guidance of lawyer Anand Grover, challenged Section 377 in the Delhi high court. Section 377, though a British colonial law codified in the Indian Penal Code in 1860 to prosecute individuals having 'carnal intercourse against the order of nature'[5] continued well into the twenty-first century, and has been used to intimidate and harass the LGBTQ+ community. The 2001 petition was the very first to challenge it. Soon, over ten NGOs and groups in Delhi came together in support of Naz, as Voices Against 377.

Anand Grover's presence and support helped Naz in many other ways too. He became the lawyer who could protect their work from police interference. Anand's contributions to the LGBTQ+ movement through his work with Naz Foundation is arguably the most important of any lawyer in India. Speaking about his association during the 377 case in particular, Anjali said, 'The kind of research that has gone into it and the kind of dedication he's shown has been tremendous.'[6]

However, it took another six years before the Delhi High Court, in 2009, toned down Section 377, stating that consensual and private sex between two adults would not be prosecuted as it violated the constitutional principles of non-discrimination on the basis of sex and the right to health. A first-hand observer of the court proceedings said, 'an audible gasp went around the room. By the time the Chief Justice had finished reading the conclusion of the judgment, people were openly weeping and there were handshakes and hugs all around.'[7] Although the 2009 judgment didn't strike down 377, this was truly a landmark moment for the LGBTQ+ community.

The victory was, however, short-lived. In 2013, the Supreme Court overturned the 2009 order. Speaking about it, Anjali said, 'It is a reflection of what we are doing with our minorities. Be it in Kashmir, be it in the North East, be it rights for the sexual minority, or animal rights, it is the same attitude. We are becoming more and more intolerant of each other.'[8] All individuals, she insisted, had the potential to prove themselves as contributing members of the society if they were given the space to do so. 'But if you impose your sets of right and wrong and therefore they have no right to live, then what can you expect from people?'[9] It would take almost a decade for Section 377 to be overturned again in a separate case. (See Menaka Guruswamy and Arundhati Katju.)

Anjali's remarkable work received worldwide attention, bringing her several accolades. In 2001, she won the Commonwealth Award and in 2007, the Government of India presented her with the Woman Achiever Award. In 2012, she was named one of *Time* magazine's 100 Most Influential People in the World. And in 2013, she was conferred the highest French order of merit, the Chevalier de la Légion d'Honneur.

Over the years, the focus on HIV and LGBTQ+ issues has pushed Naz to embrace various programmes aimed at prevention, care, changing mindset and empowering families. Beyond her work through Naz, Anjali also set up an animal sanctuary called All Creatures Great and Small in Silakhari, Haryana, in 2012.

Anjali's resilience and heart for others speaks volumes. At a time when HIV/AIDS was considered contagious, just by touch, she became a guardian angel to all those whose lives were at the greatest risk. She has changed a billion minds, championing LGBTQ+ rights for more than thirty years. Anjali's story is a poignant reminder that our activism should extend beyond the realm of online expressions and keyboard warrior status. Her tireless efforts to challenge oppressive laws inspire us to embrace empathy, stand up against injustice and create a more inclusive India – where every voice is different and unique.

Ashok Row Kavi

The Mother of the Gay Community

From being a monk to 'mother' to the gay community – Ashok Row Kavi has lived many lives. A larger-than-life figure, Ashok is India's first gay rights activist, the founder of The Humsafar Trust, India's first and leading LGBTQ+ NGO and a pioneer of HIV/AIDS outreach programmes in India in the 1990s and 2000s, especially for gay men. In this book alone, he plays a significant cameo in two other stories, a testament to the impact he has made in the LGBTQ+ community.

Ashok was born in 1947 to a poor couple in Bombay who were 'economic refugees'[1] from Karnataka. 'Mom says I was born under a staircase although last minute she had an institutional delivery in a hospital,'[2] according to Ashok. His father worked as a projectionist at the Imperial

Cinema. This early exposure to Bollywood shaped Ashok greatly. 'I was also born on the sets of Bollywood. I knew everything about Bollywood. But the important part is, there was also a gay side to Bollywood. I still remember *Screen* talking about how a particular actor had gone to ask for Shyama's hand to her mother, who said, "Look beta! I'm so grateful but . . . you must first give divorce to Akhtar, your driver!" Wonderful gossip like that, which everybody took it in stride. It wasn't a big deal.'[3]

As he grew up, Ashok began to sense that he was different. He would often go to his neighbour's house to play with their son. 'He and I used to be always together playing "doctor-doctor" and look at each other's thermometers,'[4] he remembers with a laugh. By the time he entered adolescence, the bullying started too as he was conspicuously different from the rest. Despite that, he managed to finish school – A levels at that time – at the young age of sixteen and enter college. He attended several colleges in Bombay, eventually enrolling in an engineering course. But his resilience was short-lived. Fleeing away from the reactions to his homosexuality, Ashok joined the Ramakrishna Mission to become a monk and study theology.

The experience shaped Ashok and gave him the courage and the right guidance to confront his homosexuality. 'It showed me that sex wasn't an issue, it's been made a problem,' he said.[5] He owes it to a senior monk, a 'truly evolved human being'[6] who 'unveiled'[7] his homosexuality, making it 'painless and worthy of all that is great in man's heritage.'[8] Ashok left the monastery and headed to Berlin to study journalism at the International School of Journalism.

After returning, Ashok worked as a journalist at the *Indian Express, The Free Press Journal, Sunday Mail, The Daily* and *The Week*. In 1971, Ashok joined his friend Anthony Van Braband to edit *Debonair*, an Indian men's magazine on the lines of *Playboy*. Its content raised many eyebrows. 'It was quite pathbreaking that a girly magazine aimed at cishet men was being brought out by two gay men,' he told *Man's World*.[9]

In 1986, he grabbed the headlines in a sensational 'coming-out' interview with *Savvy* magazine. In the same magazine, his mother, Shobha Row Kavi, also gave an interview, becoming the first Indian mother to speak about her son's sexual orientation to the media.

By 1986, the AIDS epidemic had begun to cover India under its veil. The same year, Ashok attended Montreal's fifth international AIDS conference. He was astounded to see activists and health workers in the West battling for money for treatment. Ashok wondered what would happen in India, where there were vast networks of men who were having sex with other men but a complete absence of a homosexual community.

Several factors made the spread of HIV complex in India. These included limited awareness and understanding of the disease, social stigma, cultural and religious taboos, lack of access to healthcare and prevention services and high levels of poverty and inequality. Societal attitudes and discrimination against marginalized communities, such as sex workers, men having sex with men and transgender individuals, further compounded the challenges. The LGBTQ+ community in India were already facing widespread stigma. The AIDS epidemic only intensified this discrimination.

In 1989, Ashok began to work at the Asha Project, a Municipal Eye Hospital in Kamathipura that mostly served sex workers. Jairaj Thanekar, a very progressive municipal commissioner, led the Bombay Municipal Corporation in organizing sex workers. Together with Ashok, he started to conduct outreach activities. It was during this period that Ashok came to the realization that he wanted to be a gay activist.

In 1990, Ashok started India's first and only gay magazine, *Bombay Dost*, with the core message of social mobilization of sexual minorities. The first-ever article on Section 377 and how it would affect the HIV/AIDS outreach programmes was published in the magazine, written by one of Mumbai's well-known criminal lawyers, Shrikant Bhatt. It was a newsletter that served as a lifeboat for many gay men bringing up subjects such as anal STIs and AIDS,'[10] Ashok said, talking to the *Man's World*.

But there were many issues beyond the purview of a magazine. To meet this need, Ashok along with a few friends like Shridhar Rangayan and Suhail Abbasi started The Humsafar Trust in April 1994. Its goal was to reach out to the LGBTQ+ community in Mumbai Metro and surrounding areas. Jairaj Thanekar once again took a proactive role and allotted them a drop-in centre. Ashok and friends started a clinic in the space for free counselling and antiretroviral therapy (ART), a treatment to cure the illness or slow down the advancement process. It was the first openly gay community-based organization to be allotted space in a municipal building in Mumbai.

'We used to collect samples and send them to government hospitals. That is how our first outreach program for AIDS and HIV started. It was also the first centre for gay men that united gay men from all castes, communities and backgrounds. We were even visited by transwomen (the hijra community) who also dealt with sexual problems. We were teaching all of them about checking themselves for any physical symptoms of STIs and STDs,' said Ashok.[11]

The Humsafar Trust started as an HIV/AIDS health service centre for gay men, but it soon opened itself up to all of the LGBTQ+ community, offering them guidance, checkups, hospital referrals, confidential HIV testing, counselling and outreach. Within a few years, the trust had provided health services to over 60,000 men.

Something that started as a little idea has over the years pulsated into a vision that Ashok never thought would be possible. The Humsafar Trust stayed true to its meaning and emerged as a safety net for the Indian queer community.

Alongside his work in the trust, Ashok has been a prominent figure on the global stage, representing the voices of the LGBTQ+ community at numerous international forums and conferences. He extensively covered the AIDS pandemic and as a result of his reporting for prominent publications, he was elected as a delegate to the Amsterdam International AIDS Conference. He also served as the chairperson of the Second International Congress on AIDS. In order to 'track the illness and warn young gay men about the risk,'[12] Ashok created questionnaires for the Centre for AIDS

Prevention Studies at the University of California, San Francisco, in 1998.

For his work, his larger-than-life persona, he is known among the gay community as 'Amma'. 'Those people might have seen some leadership qualities in me,'[13] he said of the nickname. After devoting almost three decades to The Humsafar Trust, he stepped down as chair of the board of trustees in 2020.

Today, at the age of seventy-six, the veteran activist still remains active. He mentors younger gay men and has started a group called Mumbai Seenagers for senior gay and bisexual men who need support as they grow old. He also teaches in various academic institutions and corporates about sex, sexuality and gender. Above all, he continues to be the Amma of the queer community in India.

Laxmi Narayan Tripathi

The Transformer

At six feet, decked up in striking colours and heavy makeup, Laxmi Narayan Tripathi commands unwavering attention. Like the title of her autobiographical narrative *Me Hijra, Me Laxmi*, her every move punctuates her identity as Laxmi the hijra, pushing the viewer to think beyond the two slots of gender. Like she wears her identity on her sleeve, she wears her activism too, and she has been one of the loudest voices in the country against the discrimination of transgenders. When Salman Rushdie went to Thane in Maharashtra to meet her, she came across as 'a hijra of extreme articulacy and force of character.'[1]

As a child, Laxmi despised the hijra community and always wondered why they stripped and clapped their hands on the streets. Little did Laxmi know that years

later, she would become the first transgender person
to represent the Asia Pacific region at the UN. When
we think of hijras, we imagine them knocking on our
car doors asking for money or coming home during a
wedding for a gift, but Laxmi was much, much more. She
was one of the few hijras of the '90s who learnt English
and acquired a college education, and became the face
of the community. Today, as everyone knows, Laxmi is
a media celebrity. But she had to come a long way to
become Laxmi.

Laxmi was born in 1978 in Thane to an orthodox
Brahmin family. When she was six years old, she developed
an interest in Bharatanatyam – later she would acquire a
postgraduate degree in the dance form. Initially, Laxmi's
father was against her learning to dance. Her father's first
cousin and her teachers encouraged him to let the child
pursue dancing. And her father grudgingly relented.

Laxmi recalls from her growing years, 'As I was
growing up, in the eyes of the world and those of my
own family, I never gravitated towards "manly" things.
I loved to draw and paint, twirl around in lovely, flowy
fabric, and wear make-up and jewellery. My absolute
passion, however, was dance. In dancing, I was completely
and utterly free. All of this meant, of course, that I was
feminine. But the problem was that I was feminine

despite being a boy. So when I wore bangles because they looked so good, red and shiny on my wrists, I would be told off by my friend's mother. Everyone's reactions around me seemed to indicate that I was acting like a girl, so I felt like a girl too. I would often refer to myself as one – "Main abhi aati hoon,"[2] I would say, and immediately be reprimanded for doing that. "Ladkiyon jaisi harkat mat kar (Don't act like girls)," I would be told. When I decided to grow my hair because long hair is beautiful, it really disturbed my father. He made sure I had it cut because "Achche ghar ke ladke aise nahi karte (Boys from good households do not behave this way)."[3]

It wasn't just dancing. Laxmi grew up wanting to put on lipstick and wrap herself in her mother's saris. She was totally oblivious that she was different from an early age and always thought of herself just like any other child. But everyone around her started calling her 'Mamu … Chakka … Hijra',[4] at a young age and then she began to feel she was not normal.

From facing sexual abuse to being ostracized for her effeminate nature and her love for dancing, Laxmi experienced it all in her growing-up years. But if there was one trait that stood by her, it was her resolve to never be afraid. This resolve helped her to not only stand up for herself but scores like her. In the later days, she would often echo the line from the famous song 'Good girls go to heaven (Bad girls go everywhere)'[5] to sum up herself. 'I discovered that passivity did not pay. It might endear me to society, but it came with a price. I decided at that moment to raise my voice against the things I did not like. Henceforth, I would not do anything against my will,' said Laxmi.[6]

When she was about ten years old, Laxmi found herself at the cruising park Maheshwari Udyan at King's Circle in Mumbai, where hijras and kothis (effeminate homosexual men) regularly met in the evening on the weekends, spent some happy moments in each other's company and returned home. It was the same park where she first met the activist Ashok Row Kavi (see essays on Ashok Row Kavi and The Friendship Walk). A teenage Laxmi had begun to question her identity and Ashok was the first to assure her that she was normal. Encouraging Laxmi to focus on her studies, Ashok told her to stay away from the garden and think about school and her future. Ashok would continue to play a crucial role in Laxmi's life and also become close to her mother.

As Laxmi finished school, she continued to question her identity. She wasn't just gay like the men who came to Maheshwari. She would show up wearing hot pants, long T-shirts, kurtas with huge dupattas, steel bangles, nose rings and red lipstick to cruising parks but felt ostracized by the gay community because of her appearance. Nor did she feel a sense of belonging with the drag queen community. She was neither gay nor a drag queen; she believed that she was a woman.

Laxmi started visiting the hijra gharanas in Sonapur, Maharashtra, where she met hijras who were involved in sex work. 'Yeh saari mai koi maja nahi hai' (There's no fun in any of this), said the hijras, warning Laxmi to never become a hijra.

In 1998, when Laxmi was working as a model coordinator, she met a hijra called Shabina. Shabina was the sibling of her friend, a model. It was the beginning of a long friendship. Shabina served as a guide and mentor, someone who helped her navigate the hijra world, learn about the history of the community, the intricacies of its rituals, the concepts of chelas, gurus and gharanas. In her book *Red Lipstick: The Men in My Life,* she talks about going to Shabina's Lashkar gharana, the head of whom was Lata Naik: 'Nervous and unsure, I finally gathered the courage to ask those assembled there, "I want to become a chela. How much is the fee?" To my surprise, they all burst out laughing. Lata guru, who went on to become my guru, said, "There is no fee, child. If you want to become my chela, come." My initiation ceremony, the *reet*, followed

31

soon after – I was given two green saris, which are known as *jogjanam* saris signifying the inculcation into a new way of life and crowned with the community dupatta.'[7]

Soon after, Laxmi became a bar dancer. However, this was short-lived as Maharashtra home minister R.R. Patil decided in 2005 to shut down the city's dance bars putting numerous underprivileged women and the drag/gay community out of work. Laxmi organized several protests against this move. The dancers lost, but Laxmi got her first taste of activism.

A few years later, Shabina disappeared, her disappearance remained a mystery and created a void in Laxmi's life for a long time and she joined the hijra community. That was the point when Laxmi's life fell into place.

Laxmi experienced many obstacles as she transitioned from one life to another, but it was the hijra community where she eventually sought solace and felt authentic. It was a colossal shift in her life, from being a gay man to becoming a hijra. When she became a hijra, the majority of her friends moved away from her, leaving her abandoned. The gay community never accepted her, and drag queens thought she was too cheap.

'When I became a hijra, a great burden was lifted off my head. I felt relaxed. I was now neither a man nor a woman. I was a hijra. I had my own identity. No longer did I feel like an alien.'[8] However, her mother's reaction was completely different. 'As we entered the house, mother began to beat her breasts and wail loudly, as if there was a death in the family. Perhaps it was the most spontaneous way to react when confronted by the news that the scion of the family has become a hijra.'[9]

Members of the Indian hijra community have frequently suffered abuse or been coerced into sex work. The struggle for equality, dignity and inclusion for India's third gender has benefited from Laxmi's notoriety. When Ashok Row Kavi started to appeal Section 377 of the Indian Penal Code, which made homosexuality a crime, Laxmi joined his team in the early 2000s. She attended the inaugural gathering at the press club in full make-up and spoke in English. Her appearance – she looked ferocious with her black-kohl-lined eyes and bold red lipstick – and her ability to speak in English attracted the press. This was only the beginning. Laxmi was soon going to become the public face of the hijra community.

But despite coming out, Laxmi still had personal battles to wage. When she gave her first interview to Zee News, there was panic in her house. Her family made attempts to marry her off and made alternative suggestions like getting her married to a woman; anything to fix her.

One day she told her father, in frustration, that if he forced her to marry a woman, she would run away from home or castrate herself. After that day, her parents didn't say anything to her, but she was asked to restrict her TV presence, which eventually showed Laxmi that her family just wanted to protect her.

Eventually, her parents came to terms with Laxmi's identity. When her father was asked about his thoughts on Laxmi's sexuality in an interview, he responded, 'If my child was handicapped, would you even ask me whether I'd have asked him to leave home? And just because his sexual orientation is different?'[10] In *Me Hijra, Me Laxmi*, she recalled her father's response to a similar question. 'Why should I expel Laxmi from the family? I am his father, he is my responsibility. A hijra can be born to any family. If we spun them and show them the door, we leave them with no alternative but to become beggars. Driving Laxmi out of the house was out of question.'[11] Laxmi said, 'I faced a lot of physical abuse in my childhood, and there was disdain towards me too. But my parents accepted me as I was. Whatever I am today is because of them. My mother used to say, 'Desi ghee ka laddu tedha bhi sahi rahta hai.' (It's the virtues of a person, and not their looks, that define them.) [12]

In 2000, Laxmi went to Kamathipura in Mumbai for

an HIV programme where she met sex workers. She was shocked when she came to know that they had to sell their bodies for just Rs 50 and Rs 100. Her soul cried hearing their stories. That was the moment when she decided to become an activist. Now Laxmi was active, fighting against social injustices and all kinds of prejudice. 'I felt empowered, and empowerment is not a word that normally exists in the vocabulary of a hijra. It is true that as a person, I, Laxmi Narayan Tripathi, liked taking on new challenges, but as a hijra, I was never allowed to,'[13] she would write.

Fighting her own battles from within, Laxmi said, 'If there is one role for me, the one big cause I know I am meant for, the raison d'être of my existence, it is that of an activist. I firmly believe that even if you have the best laws, unless you change the mindset of people, nothing will change. And that is what true activism means to me. That's why I can never be a 9-5 activist, I don't understand that, I am and can only be a 24/7 activist. Which is why, whatever the circumstances in my personal life, in public I have to be that – *the* Laxmi.'[14]

Laxmi broke many boundaries through her activism. She became the first chairperson of the Dai Welfare Society, the first registered organization in South Asia working for the welfare of the transgender community, and the founder of the sexual minorities' rights organization Astitva in 2007. Laxmi, in 2014, petitioned the court to include a 'third category' for transgender people on all paperwork.

National Legal Services Authority v. Union of India (2014) was a landmark judgment of the Supreme Court of India, which declared transgender people the 'third gender'. The fundamental rights granted under the Constitution of India would be equally applicable to them, it said. The judgment also gave transgender people the right to identify themselves as male, female or third gender. Given their status as socially and economically backward classes, the court declared that they would be granted reservations in admissions to educational institutions and jobs.[15]

This landmark judgment has been cited in various cases in commonwealth countries, such as Jones v. United States (2016), National Human Rights Commission v. Secretary, Ministry of Defence (2017) of Bangladesh, Canadian Armed Forces v. MacEachen (2018), Bell v. Tavistock (2020) at High court of England and Wales.

Additionally, to address the medical needs of transgender people, governments were mandated by the highest courts to build third bathrooms and establish health departments. Transgenders would be permitted to adopt kids and, following gender reassignment surgery, be able to identify as the gender of their choice. In fact, Laxmi became the first Indian transgender person to get her official documents changed and hold a passport that identified her as a transgender.

In 2008, she became the first transgender person to represent the Asia-Pacific region at the UN. 'I was no longer just Laxmi, the hijra; I was India,'[16] she said, proud and emotional to be representing her country. As she entered the General Assembly, she touched the Indian flag and became teary-eyed. She described her role as being the bridge between her transgender community and the government.

Over the years, Laxmi has had many wins. In 2011, she was a contestant on the popular reality show Bigg Boss. 'The two of them, Salman and Sanjay, always referred to me as "Laxmiji". The suffix "ji" is reserved for people worthy of respect. It has never been used for hijras,'[17] she said with pride. It was not just for her as an individual but for the community she belonged to. Laxmi had brought the hijra community to the mainstream of the Indian entertainment industry.

Laxmi continues to work for the betterment of the transgender community in India. Currently serving as 'Mahamandaleshwar, someone who has been elevated by their peers to the highest level of Hindu spiritual guardianship, she leads the Kinnar Akhara, a Hindu religious order established in 2018 by the Hijra community. The akhara showcased itself at the 2019 Kumbh Mela, and it promotes discussion on Hinduism and LGBTQ+ topics. Laxmi today wants to elevate the transgender community and restore the lost space they once had inside the Hindu faith, where they were historically considered 'demi-gods'.

Laxmi is optimistic and envisions a world where people stop using the word 'they' and start using the word 'we,' when referring to hijras. 'If I have to say goodbye to the world, at least my soul should be contented that I did something . . . I didn't build a palace, but at least I laid one stone – the foundation of rights, equality, dignity and inclusion of my community in mainstream society.'[18]

Bhupen Khakhar

A Fearless Painter

Two kinds of icons stand out visibly in this book – those
who have fought actively for LGBTQ+ rights and those
who have been extremely successful in their fields and
have been open about their sexuality, thus becoming role
models for many Indians. But there is also a third category
of people – those like filmmaker Rituparno Ghosh, who
not only have achieved success in their professions and been
open about their sexuality but have made their sexuality a
central theme of their work, thus taking LGBTQ+ issues
to a wider world. Artist Bhupen Khakhar belonged to this
category. A Padma Shri awardee, described as 'possibly the
most provocative painter in contemporary Indian art',[1] he
remains the country's most important gay artist, one who
achieved great recognition for his work both in India and

internationally and who made homosexuality a central plank of it.

Bhupen was born in 1934 in Khetwadi, Bombay. His family pressured him into a traditional career path and instead of following his dreams and heading to art school, the young man ended up studying economics, commerce and later qualified as a chartered accountant. This would be his formal profession for the next twenty-seven years of his life. Bhupen's passion for art persisted, leading him to join evening art classes at the Sir J.J. School of Art in Mumbai in 1958 while he worked as an accountant by day.

At thirty, he finally decided to plunge into art and went to Baroda University (known for its new and exciting fine arts faculty) to do his master's in art criticism encouraged by the painter, Ghulam Mohammed Sheikh. It was Sheikh who pushed him to become a painter. Bhupen eventually moved to Baroda, settling among a vibrant community of artists, which included Sheikh, Vivan Sundaram and Sunil Patwardhan – becoming a part of what is today known as the Baroda School.

He began painting in his early thirties, during the 1960s, holding his first solo exhibition in Bombay and then showing his work across the country and internationally in shows such as Art Now in India, London, Newcastle and Ghent, IX Biennale de São Paulo and the First Triennale-

India, New Delhi. It was at the Triennale in 1968 that he met the great British artist Howard Hodgkins, who was to become a lifelong friend and mentor. Hodgkins would later say of his first sighting of Bhupen's work – 'I felt they were the only ones there that were original. They had their own identity. They were three narrative pictures. Their authenticity shone out like a sound of a bell in this terrible, crowded exhibition.'[2]

Bhupen's early works reflected his experimentation with various styles and techniques. He drew inspiration from both Western art movements, such as Pop Art and Surrealism, and traditional Indian art forms, and was regarded as India's first true pop artist. His first big series – the Tradesmen series – was made in the 1970s, as a play on the nineteenth-century Company School pictures, which portrayed ordinary Indians often at their work.

In his series, Bhupen painted working-class men (some who became his friends, others lovers) – the barber, the watch repairman and even the assistant accountant he worked with. Artforum reports, 'In one, a sign announces "DE-LUXE TAILORS". In another, a doormat promises "GOOD LUCK". These paintings dip into the vernacular, even kitsch, the language of the bazaar. "Good taste can be very killing," the artist once said.'[3] In 2017, Sotheby's would sell *De-Luxe Tailors* (given by Bhupen to Hodgkins as a gift), a 1972 painting from the series, for $1.4 million.

In 1979, Bhupen spent six months in Britain working as the Bath Academy of Arts' resident artist, after which he participated in a show called 'Narrative Painting' in London. During his time in England, he saw the growing acceptability of homosexuality, a decade after it had been made legal, and interacted with the famous gay artist David Hockney. He would say how important those six months had been and that it had allowed him to see how men could live with other men.

In 1980, Bhupen's mother died after which he began to fearlessly incorporate his sexuality into his work. His paintings became his coming out. 'I did not announce it verbally, but there were paintings that related to gay subjects,'[4] he said. This groundbreaking move made Bhupen the first Indian artist to declare his homosexuality openly. His paintings, such as *You Can't Please All* and *Two Men in Benares*, presented a raw and honest portrayal of queer experiences, challenging stereotypes. The artist would say, 'I have chosen homo-eroticism as a theme because I am gay. What is happening in India – social rejection – did happen once in countries like the USA and Europe. The police in all societies have beaten up gays and lesbians. But now they have been accepted by society. For me, there is nothing unnatural about homosexuality.'[5]

Of this phase, *Two Men in Benares* (1982) is perhaps his most iconic work. The painting depicts two naked men with erect penises, embracing each other. Despite its explicitness, the atmosphere of the picture is profoundly tender and intimate. Bhupen described it and his work during this period as his attempt to create 'an iconography of homosexual love'.[6] It was sold for Rs 22 crore (£2.54 million) by Sotheby's in 2019. Despite the boldness of his work, he did feel the effect of coming out so openly. 'Now I feel amused, but at that time I felt very pressured because in India there are hardly any painters doing gay subjects . . . I felt ostracised and even my friends advised me to see a doctor,'[7] he said.

The 1980s were a time of great recognition for the artist. In 1982, Hodgkins curated an important show at the Tate Museum called 'Six Indian Artists'. They included some of the country's most important modern artists – Abanindranath Tagore, Jamini Roy, Amrita Sher-Gil, M.F. Husain and K.G. Subramanyan. Hodgkins also included Bhupen Khakhar, who went on to play another kind of role in the art world. From 1985 to 1988, he served as the honorary secretary of the Lalit Kala Akademi, India's National Academy of Art, helping promote contemporary art and support emerging artists.

During the 1990s, Bhupen delved into watercolours,

finding a new style. He was depicted as 'the accountant' in Salman Rushdie's novel *The Moor's Last Sigh*. In return, Bhupen painted a portrait of the author titled *The Moor*, which hangs today in the National Portrait Gallery in London. In 1992, he became the first Indian artist to be selected for the prestigious Documenta IX.

In his final years, Bhupen Khakhar focused on a series of paintings set in Ahmedabad. Living in Baroda, he also experienced the 2002 communal riots and created numerous large-scale artworks in response, which would be shown internationally. He would die the year after, in August 2003, at the age of sixty-nine, a month after the death of his companion, Vallarbhai Shah.

Bhupen's paintings today can be encountered in numerous public collections, including the Metropolitan Museum of Art in New York, as well as in various private collections worldwide. His artworks have been prominently showcased in exhibitions across India and globally and in 2019, he was the subject of a solo show at the Tate Modern – one of the few Indian artists to have been accorded this honour.

Bhupen Khakhar's contributions as an artist and his advocacy for LGBTQ+ visibility have left an enduring imprint on the art world. Through his artistry, he broke barriers, sparked conversations and paved the way for greater acceptance and understanding of diverse identities. He will be remembered as a fearless artist who used his brush to create a more inclusive and empathetic world.

Saleem Kidwai and Ruth Vanita

Ammunition for the LGBTQ+ community

Saleem Kidwai and Ruth Vanita are renowned scholars and activists who edited a pioneering book called *Same-Sex Love in India: Readings from Literature and History*, which dove deep into two millennia of Indian history to document same-sex love. Not only did the book became the foundation for Indian gay studies, it was also used by lawyers to argue for the removal of Section 377 from the Indian Penal Code in the 2009 Delhi High Court case, and even cited by the Supreme Court in the landmark 2018 judgment. There are many great books in the world – but it's rare to find a book such as this that has had such an impact in the real world.

Saleem was born in 1951 in Lucknow. At a young age, he realized that something about him did not fit into a heteronormative world. He was seventeen when he left Lucknow, restless and full of curiosity, eventually going on to study history at St Stephen's College. He earned his master's degree in 1973, and Delhi University recruited him as a history lecturer.

In 1976, Saleem went to Canada to do a PhD in Islamic History at McGill University, mainly seeking the freedom to be gay. It opened up a whole new world of people he could align with. The gay bars and discos acquainted him with friends, lovers, drag queens and transgenders. These spaces offered him companionship and he spent many precious days meeting people, making merry. This world, however, came crashing one day when the police suddenly raided the gay bar he was in with his friends. The violence that followed left Saleem traumatized and he returned to India in 1981, abandoning his studies.

In the 1980s, while teaching at Ramjas College in Delhi as an associate professor of medieval and Mughal history, he met someone like him. Ruth Vanita was a gender and sexuality studies scholar with specialization in British and Indian literary history. Ruth had co-founded the women's group Manushi, which soon started publishing a feminist journal by the same name, publishing articles on women and society backed by academic research and grassroots activism. She co-edited *Manushi* from 1979 to 1991 for no remuneration.

Ruth and Saleem were the first scholars at Delhi University to introduce queer themes and perspectives in their classes. Students were often shocked by their unconventional take on history and literature. The idea of writing the book together came in 1994. The two had independently been collecting texts that talked of same-sex desire and love. Ruth in Sanskrit and Indian vernacular languages and Saleem in Urdu, Persian and Arabic. 'As you'd be reading, you'd find lots of things that would strike you, and your gaydar would start tingling ... Both Ruth and I had been doing similar things,'[1] Kidwai said.

They decided to co-edit an anthology of queer literature of India with texts culled from the classical era and to contemporary India. They drew up a list of writings they already knew about and started looking for other material. At the time, queer studies as a discipline was still alien to India.

When *Same-Sex Love* arrived, it became the first ever book to deal with Indian written traditions of homoerotic love and one that showed comprehensively that Indian homosexuality, and the ways in which it was talked about, had historically a strong tradition in the country and was not a 'recent' or 'modern' import.

The book, in four parts, examined how romantic and passionate relationships between men and women have been portrayed in Indian history using literature and mythology. The first part explored Hindu and Buddhist traditions through ancient Sanskrit and Pali texts. It included extracts from the epic, classical and early Puranic periods, from the 2 BCE to the 8 CE. The second and third parts focused on the medieval period, with the second section looking at Sanskritic tradition and the third section examining Perso-Urdu tradition. The final discussed modern Indian texts.

The first section of the book looked at patterns and tropes in literature from the classical period, including friendships that culminated in celibacy, sex change, cross-dressing, the undoing of gender and children being born miraculously to parents of the same sex. There were punishments for partaking in homoerotic activities, the introductory chapter of this section reveals.

The second part of *Same-Sex Love* looked at the literature produced under the Islamic culture in India between the eighth and the eighteenth centuries. The texts produced during this period were in Sanskrit, Sanskrit-based languages, south Indian languages and in Perso-Arabic and Urdu tradition. In the first three groups, the texts chosen for *Same-Sex Love* included the

Puranas, vernacular retellings of epic and Puranic stories, Katha literature, historical chronicles produced in the courts and devotional poetry. Writing in the book about devotional literature of medieval India in particular, Ruth said 'Bhakti' was 'a movement of the oppressed'[2] where it allowed for 'the direct and loving relationship of the devotee with a personal god.'[3] It allowed for anyone to assume an intimate relationship with a chosen deity, in multiple forms – as a friend, spouse or child – affording an easy transition through gender roles.

The third section, on Perso-Urdu literature, traced the history of this literature. Saleem wrote about how armed migrants in the end of the tenth century, who entered India from beyond the Hindukush mountains eventually marking the establishment of kingdoms ruled by Muslims in country, brought with them Perso-Turko-Arabic cultural traditions. Homoeroticism figured visibly in these Muslim medieval histories and in favourable light, which Saleem attributed to the possible 'cosmopolitanism of urban Islamic culture'.[4] By the seventeenth century, Urdu emerged as the high literary language, replacing Persian. 'Medieval poetry depicts romantic and erotic interactions between men across class and religious divides,'[5] wrote Saleem in his introduction to the medieval texts in the Perso-Urdu tradition. Even the roles of the wife and the lover, irrespective of the latter's gender, were 'defined and distinguished'.[6]

The final section of *Same-Sex Love* focused on modern India, defined by the editors for the purposes of the book as the nineteenth and twentieth centuries. This period was characterized by two significant phenomena: the emergence of the 'minor homophobic voice',[7] largely ignored in the pre-colonial mainstream society, into a 'dominant voice'[8] and the depiction of sexual love between women more explicitly than before, even as such love between men went under wraps.[9] However, a clear dictum against homosexuality came in 1861 with the introduction of Section 377 of the Indian Penal Code, marking a retrogressive shift in India's homoerotic tradition. Besides this law, the vocal denouncement of Indian social and sexual practices by the British educators and missionaries, guided by their Victorian values of 'deep antipleasure and antisex bias'[10], impacted the way the social reform movements shaped up in that period. Homophobia made its way into the mindset of many educated Indians.

Ruth and Saleem also covered India's contemporary period and concluded by discussing the treatment of homosexuality in India post the 1990s, particularly in relation to print and electronic media and film.

When the book was initially presented to Indian

publishers, they declined because they thought it would be explosive. It was published by the American publisher St Martin's Press in 2000.

The book became a foundational source for queer studies in India. In an email to the *Washington Post* in 2021, Shohini Ghosh, a professor at the A.J.K. Mass Communication Centre, Jamia Millia Islamia, India, said, 'During the time that the book was first published, it was commonly asserted by homophobic cultural nationalists that homosexuality was never a part of Indian tradition.'[11] To those who had an understanding of queer love, the book offered a reconfirmation of its existence in the vibrant history of South Asia. But to many, it also served as an eye-opener. It raised a few discordant notes, especially concerning some of Saleem's claims in the book.

Poet and teacher Hoshang Merchant described Saleem as 'indisputably the intellectual voice of India's gay history, especially its Urdu literature and Muslim life.'[12]

Akhil Katyal, a Delhi-based poet, while reviewing Ruth Vanita's book *The Broken Rainbow* alludes to his encounter with *Same-Sex Love*. 'I don't remember precisely when I first got hold of the book but I remember its lightning strike. I remember how its cheap photocopy became one of my most precious student possessions. It was like some strangers had handed me – someone then gingerly stepping into his own queerness – a family heirloom. In here, my ancestors could now range from a Mughal king who became "humbled and wretched and love-sick" for a boy in a bazaar, to surprising friends from the Panchatantra, crocodiles and apes, crows, and tortoises whose mutual embraces felt better than "sandal-paste blended with chill camphor" or "snowflakes delightfully cool". This work's quiet importance to scores of the subcontinent's queer lives cannot be overstated.'[13]

For lawyer Anand Grover, who represented Naz Foundation in its 377 battles (see Anjali Gopalan), the book became a bible. 'Saleem Kidwai and Ruth Vanita were the ammunition for us to advocate what our history was and how our culture was and how to reclaim it . . . The mainstream history and for the vast majority of the people, the thinking was that Section 377 is part of our culture, and they had no idea that prior to the British it was a different ballgame,'[14] he said. It was also cited in the landmark 2018 Supreme Court judgment, describing *Same-Sex Love in India* as a book that demonstrated, 'that same-sex love has flourished, evolved and been embraced in various forms since ancient times.'[15]

Saleem suffered a cardiac arrest on 30 August 2021 and died in a hospital in Lucknow. His long-time friend

Sunil Gupta, reminisced about how they talked a lot about where one could live as a gay man at that time, and how Saleem opted to live in India and make a difference.[16]

Saleem's demise unquestionably leaves a void in queer scholarship and the larger LGBTQ+ community in India that will never be filled, at least not for a very long time. There are many activists, poets, authors, educators, filmmakers and attorneys in India's queer community. But if there is anything we don't have enough of, it's historians. We can only hope that someone will come forward to carry on Saleem Kidwai's legacy. Meanwhile, Ruth Vanita now serves as the programme director of South and South East Asian Studies at the University of Montana. Her writings extend beyond academia; she has written novels and short stories. These works offer compelling narratives that humanize and celebrate the experiences of LGBTQ+ individuals, challenging societal norms and prejudices.

Wendell Rodricks

More than a Designer

To love someone, to have a job that one feels passionately about and to live in the countryside with nature – Wendell Rodricks achieved all that he ever wanted in his life. The well-known designer was one of the few men in the fashion industry who publicly embraced his sexuality, even when homosexuality was criminalized in India. He would come out on national television in 2002, arguably the first Indian to come out on television. 'I did it to show the younger generation that it was possible to have a long love life and celebrate it rather than hiding in the closet or behind a facade', he said.[1] Wendell was proud of his sexuality, and being a celebrity, he wanted the next generation to be proud as well.

Wendell was born in 1960, in a Goan Catholic family

living in Mahim, Bombay. He knew from his early pubescence that he liked boys. While the other boys were noticing the other sex, his interest lay somewhere else. He would later say that growing up gay in the seventies and eighties of India was 'sheer cold terror'[2].

In 1982, with a degree in catering, Wendell started his first job in Muscat, Oman, working for the Royal Oman Police Officer's Club. During the course of his job, Wendell met his husband Jerome Marrel through mutual friends. They got together right after their first date. Almost twenty years on, in 2002, Wendell and Jerome formalized their union in India, under the French law, 'Pacte Civil de Solidarité'. Though the union took place under foreign law and in a French embassy, it was also the first same-sex union to be formalized on the soil of India. 'It wasn't a romantic decision but an assertion of our rights,' said Wendell of that decision.[3] He wanted the same rights as any heterosexual married couple – such as filing taxes together, migrating to countries that recognized same-sex marriage, or signing off for each other on serious medical procedures.

It was then that he came out on TV. His family did not respond well. In his memoir *The Green Room*, Wendell writes that none of them came for Christmas lunch that year. Jerome and Wendell went to bed heartbroken and in despair as 'forty kilos of pork lay cooling on the buffet table.'[4]

Wendell always prioritized love in his life; his sexual orientation was not about physical attraction alone. 'People feel sexuality is only about the physical. Far from it. For me it was the romance of an intellectual connection,'[5] he would say. The *Indian Express* declared the two could well have been 'India's first official gay couple.'[6] Firstpost said, 'By being out as a couple, Wendell Rodricks and Jerome Marrel gave us an image of the possibility of a domestic life together that happened to be gay.'[7]

The relationship also proved to be a professional turning point for Wendell and encouraged him to explore his creative side and pursue a career in design. He started saving for his education in fashion and abandoned his hospitality career. Between 1986 and 1988, Wendell studied fashion in London and Paris. He launched his own label in 1989 with his first show held at the Regal Room of the Oberoi Hotel in Mumbai. The successes came from there. He became the first Indian designer to be invited to IGEDO, the world's largest garment fair in 1995; the first Indian designer to open the Dubai Fashion Week in 2001; and was also invited to present at the Paris Prêt-à-Porter salon in 2007.

In the initial years, he operated his business from

Mumbai though he really wanted to move to Goa and live his life there. His dream did come true, though the circumstances that led to it were painful. After the collapse of the Babri Masjid in 1992, Mumbai saw heavy communal rioting. It was a violent and frightening time. Tawqir, Wendell's tailor, arrived at his home one day, anxious and out of breath.

Tawqir would commute daily by bicycle from a distant New Bombay neighbourhood called Kandivali. The terrified tailor told Wendell, 'They came to kill us. Took off a tile from our roof and threw a flaming torch into the house.'[8] Wendell recalled the moment vividly in his book *The Green Room*. Tawqir wanted to leave the city, and Wendell offered him a home in Goa. Soon after, in 1993, Wendell himself moved with his parents to Colvale, a quiet Goan village, and Tawqir installed his sewing machine on the upper floor.

Moving to Goa and setting up a business there was not a difficult task for Wendell. He was going back to his roots and was even offered a place to set his store up by a friend called Abel DeSouza, who was planning to move to Yemen. He offered to rent his place out to Wendell, which the designer gladly accepted. However, for Abel, it did not go well. The travel agent who was supposed to send Abel to Yemen duped him. Wendell wondered whether he should develop his studio or give Abel his place back. In a twist of fate, Abel, who became fascinated by Wendell's work, gave up dentistry and joined the staff as a manager.

'On D-day, I was busy hanging clothes and arranging footwear, yoga mats and bags on the steps in the boutique's corners. The wrought-iron forms carved beautifully by Vernon Arainha were draped with silk scarves and stoles. The shop was like a little jewel – warm, inviting and with a great ambience. Even now, years later, I feel that it was a beautiful shop,'[9] he wrote. Jerome, Wendell's partner, contributed funds to fly journalists to the event.

Wendell's first collection from Goa earned him the title 'Guru of Minimalism' and his next collection in 1995 pioneered the concept of 'resort wear' – a collection that arrives before the Spring/Summer collections, typically centering around vacation dressing – and 'eco-friendly' garments, at a time when the words were little-known in India. Pineapple leaves and banana stalks were boiled to distil their fibres. It was a new statement in fashion using natural fabric. He also went on to experiment with wheat and cotton.

Wendell Rodricks spent more than three decades at the pinnacle of fashion and is regarded today as the man who popularized resort fashion in the country. He saw fashion as more than a visual statement, incorporating the idea of utility and sustainability while also taking it to the next level. His work revolved around the idea of nature and culture, playing with big ideas, but they were also consistently wearable.

He was a master showman. To produce cinematic moments on the runway, Wendell pushed the frontiers of fashion and art. In one show in 2003, model Dipti Gujral donned a saree gown with an aquarium corset. *Mid-day* would say of it, 'The image went viral before it was even a thing.'[10]

Later in his career, around 2010, Wendell began to explore the idea of incorporating local handlooms into fashion. This led to his Kunbi Saree collection of 2010, where the designer showcased the attire of indigenous Kolis at Wills Lifestyle India Fashion Week. He received a standing ovation for the show and this is how the Kunbi saree reached politicians like Sonia and Priyanka Gandhi and the former President of India Pratibha Patil.

Wendell was honoured with the Padma Shri, the fourth-highest civil award of India, in 2014 for his Visionnaire Collection for visually impaired people. Soon after, Wendell decided to concentrate on his projects, including The Moda Goa Museum. So he handed over his brand to his protégé Schulen Fernandes in October 2016 and restricted his role to overseeing the collections.

When the Supreme Court overturned the earlier verdict involving Section 377, an elated Wendell announced it was time to celebrate. He started a helpline for the LGBTQ+ community with Ruby Almeida, the co-chair of Rainbow Catholics India.

Parmesh Shahani, the LGBTQ+ inclusion consultant, remembers Wendell's impact on gay life. When Parmesh wrote *Gay Bombay*, Wendell was one of the first to read it and he wrote a heartwarming blurb. Wendell, he said, was one of the kindest human beings he knew, a generous mentor who always provided him with a safe place whenever he visited Goa. Parmesh acknowledged how Wendell and his husband Jerome had been tremendously inspiring to him. And to many others like him. 'They were such an inspiration. It gave me and a generation of young gay people hope, to have such a template: that one could live with a partner, be married to them. By living an open and unapologetic life, they helped us imagine such a life for ourselves,' Shahani said.[11]

The Moda Goa Museum, which houses Goa's clothing, artefact and accessory traditions, can be found in Casa Dona Maria, Jerome and Wendell's original Goa home. To create the museum, he had to move out to a smaller house. Wendell wanted to create an intimate feeling similar to that found in a home; the museum has a library, primarily from his own collection, of books on the development of costumes and fashion and a café famous for its fish curry-rice.

Wendell Rodricks passed away at his residence in Goa on 12 February 2020. His mentee, Masaba Gupta, remembers Wendell's contribution. 'From being an admirer to a student to finally becoming his muse. He taught me to keep my heart open in what can be a terrifying industry sometimes. And open it shall always be. Open, fearless and childlike.'[12] A trailblazing designer, a queer rights activist and an environmentalist, Wendell Rodricks created more than just beautiful clothes.

Vikram Seth

A Suitable Boy

We have many achievers in India who are privately gay but have chosen not to come out publicly. As a result, apart from the extraordinary activist community in our country, young Indians have very few gay role models to look up to, who have achieved in their own professions – a top gay CEO, actor or politician. This is why Vikram Seth is a rare bird. He is one of India's most successful and acclaimed writers who also happens to be openly gay. Even before he officially came out, his novels and poetry openly discussed LGBTQ+ themes, and he has also been a vocal crusader for the decriminalization of gay sex.

Vikram was born in Kolkata in 1952. His father, Prem, was an executive of Bata, the Czech-owned shoe company. Vikram's mother, Leila, trained in law in London and she subsequently became the first female high court judge in India. As a child, Vikram enjoyed browsing through his mother's law books, and one day, he came across Section 377, a colonial law at that time that criminalized homosexuality in India.

'I read the description of what the section actually meant, and I realized it even included, if you can believe it, oral sex between a husband and wife. A crazy law like this has no place on our books. And of course, a law that is selectively used is in one aspect even worse than a law that is generally used because it puts a lot of power in individuals' hands and makes government a rule not of laws but of people.'[1]

Vikram's father took another job in 1954 and the whole family moved to England for three years. It was then that Vikram's mother passed her bar exam, placing first in the whole of England. The family (Vikram has two younger siblings, a brother and a sister) moved back to India in 1957 and lived for seven years in Patna. During his formative years (1961–67), Vikram was sent to the prestigious Doon School.

He had divided feelings about the place: appreciation for the superb education he received but a lingering bitterness toward his classmates, a bitterness that came from having been bullied there. To deal with his difficulties, he immersed himself in music and literature and became the editor-in-chief of the *Doon School Weekly*.

Vikram began his writing career as a poet. He published his first volume of poetry, called *Mappings*, in 1980. 'My father was not a very literary person, but my mother used to write poetry when she was young. There were always lots of books lying around, so I suppose I was partly inspired by her. Nevertheless, despite my father's lack of interest in the arts, it was he who encouraged me to write.'[2]

His first breakthrough book was the virtuoso novel in verse, *The Golden Gate*, published in 1986. *The Golden Gate* has an openly gay subplot – Phil and Ed are attracted to each other. But guilt takes over the devout Catholic in Ed making it impossible for a relationship between them. The book was a success, getting excellent reviews and a Sahitya Akademi Award. *The New York Times* said, 'The poem is a splendid achievement, equally convincing in its exhilaration and its sadness.'[3]

But it was the publication of *A Suitable Boy*, a 1,349-page novel, in 1993 that propelled Vikram into the public limelight. Written over eight years, when he returned to India and moved in with his parents, *A Suitable Boy* took the publishing world by storm, making Vikram a global literary star. It got extraordinary reviews and became a massive bestseller in the UK that year, outselling popular writers like John Le Carré and Wilbur Smith. Years later, in 2019, BBC News would include it in their list of 100 most inspiring novels.

In its depiction of 1950s India, its wide span portraying different communities around the country, and its lightness and humour, *A Suitable Boy* remains one of the great Indian novels written in the last three decades. The acclaimed writer Khushwant Singh would say of it, 'I lived through the period and I couldn't find a flaw.'[4]

A less talked about aspect of the book is the old friendship between two of the main characters – Maan and Firoz. Their close relationship is treated tenderly, with humour, as they fall in love with 'unsuitable' women, drink and play polo and escape together during a communal riot. In one scene, as Maan winds his arms around Firoz, there is a suggestion of intimacy the two could have possibly shared. Though it stops there, the book succeeds in working on the reader's imagination.

More books followed with even larger advances. Published in 1999, his second novel, *An Equal Music*, is about the troubled love life of a violinist followed by a memoir of the marriage of his great-uncle and aunt published in 2005 titled *Two Lives*. In 2009, Vikram finalized a deal worth around £1.7 million to move his entire backlist to Penguin UK, making it the biggest deal for any subcontinent author of that time.

Until this point, Vikram had always been private about his bisexuality, hinting at it through the characters and themes in his writing. Now he began to speak openly about himself. In the 2006 *Outlook* interview, he said, 'When I realized that I had feelings for men as well as women, at first I was worried and frightened, and there was a certain amount of Who am I? Am I a criminal? and so on. It took me a long time to come to terms with myself. Those were painful years – painful then and painful to look back on.'[5]

Overcoming years of internal struggle and confusion, Vikram reflected on the painful process of coming to terms with his own identity. 'It was difficult and basically I couldn't understand it – I mean if I felt an affection or attraction for a girl, that was one thing. And if I felt an equally deep physical and emotional attraction for a boy, that was somehow considered wrong. And this as a young chap was very deeply disturbing. I couldn't see where or what I was. I could hardly come to terms with that part of myself. And if that was true of someone like me in what you might call a liberally educated family, then you can imagine how much confusion and misery it would cause someone in a less liberal family.'[6]

In 2006, he was one of the signatories (along with Nobel laureate Amartya Sen) to an open letter to the

Government of India, members of the judiciary and all citizens expressing protest against Section 377, 'the cruel and discriminatory law'[7] that made queer people susceptible to blackmail and punishment.

When the Supreme Court overturned the decriminalization of homosexuality in 2013, (See Anjali Gopalan), Vikram appeared on one of the most memorable covers of *India Today* magazine posing as a bleary-eyed, convicted criminal holding a sign that said, 'not a criminal'.[8] Inside, he had a short but powerful article on love. 'To not be able to love the one you love is to have your life wrenched away,' he wrote, 'To do this to someone else is to murder their soul.'[9] Talking to the BBC, Vikram explained why he felt compelled to write the article. 'It takes a fair amount to get me incensed,' he said. 'And a judgment which takes away the liberties of at least 50 million lesbian, gay, bisexual and transgender (LGBT) people in India is scandalous, it's inhumane and if you wish, you can remove the e at the end of that word.'[10]

For Vikram's mother, Leila, the journey to accept his sexuality was also momentous. 'It was a criminal offence then. I worried for him. I thought he is a young man and somebody could misuse it. It is something one is not normally used to. I remember reading a book called

The Well of Loneliness about two lesbians and I remember it moved me. Love is such a beautiful thing and they could not share it with anybody. I think that came back to me. I read it at seventeen and I thought how lonely a person must be if you can't share his love with other people,'[11] she said. She, too, challenged the oppressive ruling of 2013, highlighting its flawed reasoning and disregard for evidence. She wrote a piece titled 'India: You're Criminal If Gay'[12], which appeared in the prestigious *The New York Review of Books* in 2014.

Vikram has continued to speak openly about his sexuality, as did his mother in her lifetime. In 2018, at a gathering in Goa, he emphasized the importance of this cause, highlighting how the law perpetuates harassment and victimization of LGBTQ+ individuals, casting a shadow of illegality on their lives. 'It is now seen as a fundamental right that the government or any party can't bully us, and we own the right to our private lives,' he said.[13]

When the Supreme Court finally took down Section 377 in 2018, Justice Chandrachur (one of the judges on the bench) began his judgment with the beautiful words of Vikram's mother, who had said this in the context of her son: 'What makes life meaningful is love.

The right that makes us human is the right to love. To criminalize the expression of that right is profoundly cruel and inhumane. To acquiesce in such criminalization or, worse, to recriminalize it is to display the very opposite of compassion.'[14]

Ritu Dalmia

Culinary Trailblazer

It's rare to see a successful woman chef and restaurateur in India who owns a global chain of restaurants that stretches from Delhi to Dubai, Mumbai to Milan. It's even rarer for her to be openly lesbian. That's Ritu Dalmia.

Ritu was born into a Marwari business family in Kolkata in 1972. Initially involved in her family's marble stone business, she discovered her love for Italian cuisine during a sourcing trip to Italy. This experience ignited her curiosity and set her on a path to becoming a renowned chef.

'My freedom came when I was twelve, when I knew I wanted to go out and work. I'd carry my father's briefcase around, and while no one took me too seriously, I knew what I wanted to do. All my life, I have done what I wanted to do, whether it is the person I chose to love or my career. When I started in this profession, since I come from a Marwari family, I had people asking, "Will you be cooking meat, serving beer?" They saw mine as a menial job. But I've done everything on my own terms because I strongly believe that we have to discover ourselves from our mistakes.'[1]

After attending a cooking school in Sicily, Ritu came back to Delhi, armed with idealism, enthusiasm and a burning desire to teach her hometown how to savour Italian cuisine. In 1993, at just twenty-one years and with a bank balance of less than Rs 10,000, Ritu opened her first Italian restaurant, Mezza Luna, in the vibrant lanes of Hauz Khas Village in Delhi.

Mezza Luna sadly didn't work. Seeking new horizons, Ritu moved to London in 1996 and, with her partner Andy Verma, opened the city's first Indian fine-dining restaurant, Vama, on the fashionable King's Road. The venture was a resounding success, receiving rave reviews. Speaking to *India Today* about her decision, she said, 'I had financial independence and I feel that makes such a big difference. Most people don't have the freedom of choice as they are dependent on their fathers or husbands. I am impulsive and don't generally care about consequences.'[2]

However, Ritu's heart yearned for her roots, leading

her to sell her shares in the restaurant and return to Delhi in 2000. Back in her homeland, Ritu joined forces with travel executive and entrepreneur Gita Bhalla, who went on to become her partner for many years, and together they opened Diva, an Italian restaurant in Delhi's Greater Kailash II. This quickly attained fame as the city's first standalone fine-dining Italian restaurant – before that, the fine-dining establishments were always in five-star hotels. Today, Diva remains an iconic and sought-after restaurant in the city.

From thereon, Ritu's business went from strength to strength. Today she is a co-owner of six restaurants in India, three in Milan and one in Dubai. Alongside this, she has an extremely successful global catering business. She is also the author of three cookbooks and has hosted a cooking show on NDTV Good Times.

By the age of twenty-three, Ritu knew she was gay. This realization was not without any struggle. But her turmoil lasted only one week and, being the strong person that she is, Ritu was soon ready to face the truth rather than fight it. It was more important for her to be true to herself.

When she came out, her parents, though visibly shocked, said nothing and instead provided her their support and understanding, exemplified by their thoughtful gesture of sending a box of mangoes to her partner. 'I was never ashamed about it. I told my mother and I got full support from her. She accepted my partner with open arms. My partner was more of her family than I am,' said Ritu, adding, 'I had a lot of support because I myself was okay about it.'[3]

While Ritu had been openly gay among friends and family, she had rarely spoken publicly about her private life. But two judgments triggered her to come out in public. In 2009, the Delhi High Court struck down Section 377 (see the essay on Anjali Gopalan) and decriminalized gay sex. In 2013, this judgment was overturned by the Supreme Court, which termed gay sex 'unnatural'. 'I am a well-known person. I have brought a lot of fame to India. I have made my country proud. I pay my taxes. I give employment to three hundred people. Why should I be considered a criminal? This was not acceptable to me. That's why I decided to come out in the open,' Ritu asserted.[4] She felt that the unjust law would affect future generations.

In 2016, at the age of forty-five, she joined forces with four others to challenge Article 377, which criminalized homosexuality in India, through a PIL (Public Interest Litigation). 'The Constitution talks of freedom to love and then we have something as regressive as Article 377,' she said.[5] 'It's sad that when homosexuality was criminalized in 2013, the judge said he had never met a gay person in his entire life. That's why we filed the petition ... If things are to change, it has to begin with each one of us.'[6]

It was this PIL of 2016 introduced by Ritu and others that led to the Supreme Court finally overturning 377 and making homosexuality legal in India in 2018. 'It has been two and a half years of sitting on pins and needles, not knowing how things are going to turn out. But when the hearing was going on, I felt that there was a light at the end of the tunnel. And today, that light was turned into a firework,'[7] Ritu said when the verdict came.

'I was never ashamed about my sexuality. There was a lot of trolling for two and a half years. But that was a small price to pay for what I have achieved. I heard a lot of comments behind my back about my sexuality. I have always ignored it. The awareness level is definitely a lot higher than when I was growing up. Today, kids very well know that people can have different sexual orientations and don't frown upon that, and that is amazing,' Ritu would say of the two-and-a-half-year fight.[8]

The impact of Ritu's journey extended far beyond the kitchen. Her courage and resilience served as an inspiration for countless individuals struggling to find their own path to acceptance. Through her work, she paved the way for a more inclusive and progressive India, where love knows no boundaries. From her story, it is clear that her legacy will not only be defined by her culinary achievements but also by her freedom to love. With each dish she creates and each conversation she sparks, she continues to shape a society where diversity is celebrated and love is embraced in all its forms.

Menaka Guruswamy and Arundhati Katju

National Heroes

Until 2018, it was illegal to be LGBTQ+ in India. Menaka Guruswamy and Arundhati Katju, two Supreme Court lawyers, who lived a life in hiding as a gay couple for a long time, decided to challenge Section 377, a draconian law that criminalized homosexuality and had broader implications for the LGBTQ+ community in India. The duo were the torchbearers in overturning the law and fighting for equality not only for themselves but for thousands of others like them. The couple was named *Time* magazine's 100 Most Influential People of the World in 2019.

A British colonial law, Section 377, was used to indict individuals having 'carnal intercourse against the order of nature"[1] and intimidate and harass the gay and transgender community. Section 377 forced the community to live in the shadows, especially those who were unprivileged, often pushing them towards unsafe sex.

Many organizations tried to repeal 377 in court and in the first phase of the movement, it was HIV/AIDS activists who led the march arguing that the law hindered their work. The first to seek its dismissal in the court was the AIDS Bhedbhav Virodhi Andolan in 1991. The group published *Less than Gay: A Citizen's Report*, which clearly spelt out the problems with 377.

The case went on for many years and in 2001, the Naz Foundation filed a PIL in the Delhi High Court, challenging Section 377. The moment of relief and hope came in 2009 when 377 was decriminalized by the Delhi High Court but this was short-lived. In 2013, the Supreme Court reversed the 2009 ruling, upholding the criminalization of homosexuality under Section 377 (See Anjali Gopalan). That was the moment Menaka Guruswamy and Arundathi Katju decided to fight for LGBTQ+ rights. Reacting to the 2013 verdict, Menaka recounted how the judge had asked the law officer if he knew any homosexual people. And the law officer remarked how he was not that modern. For the duo, the verdict had also meant a deeply personal loss. 'It is not nice to be declared as a criminal and then return to the court to argue other cases,' said Arundathi.[2] The court, where they practised, had also told them that gay people were second-class citizens. The judge had had no imagination of what a gay Indian was. Menaka and Arundathi decided they would never let LGBTQ+ Indians be invisible again.

In 2016, the two submitted a writ petition (Navtej Singh Johar v. Union of India) on behalf of an LGBTQ+ team of five very talented and successful dancers led by Navtej Singh Johar. Journalist Shivam Vij wrote, 'This was a remarkable shift. It wasn't NGOs but LGBT people themselves saying "I am LGBT and my fundamental rights, guaranteed by the Constitution, are being violated by Section 377".'[3]

The opening of the writ petition described the petitioners through their professional success and role in mainstream society. Menaka and Arundathi's strategy was to show the petitioners not just as LGBTQ+ persons but also as successful Indians, Indians whom anyone might have encountered:

Petitioner No. 1 Navtej Singh Johar is a Sangeet Natak Akademi Award-winning Bharatnatyam dancer and Petitioner No. 2 Sunil Mehra is a senior journalist. Petitioners No. 1 and 2 live together and have been in a committed relationship since 1998. Petitioner No. 3 Ritu Dalmia is a famed restaurateur whose restaurants, TV shows and books have brought Italian cooking into homes across the country. Petitioner No. 4 Aman Nath is an expert on Indian art and culture who, together with the late Francis Wacziarg, his partner of 23 years, established the Neemrana chain of hotels to restore and preserve India's historic buildings. Petitioner No. 5 (Ayesha Kapur) worked as a successful professional in the field of marketing, and is now a consultant in the Food and Beverages Industry.[4]

Others too joined in, submitting similar petitions, thus emphasizing they were part of the larger and vibrant world of the LGBTQ+ community. The list included 'hotelier Keshav Suri; transgender rights activists Akkai Padmashali, Uma Umesh and Suma M.; a group of parents of LGBT persons, activists Harish Iyer and Ashok Row Kavi; Arif Jafar, a gay man who spent 47 days in jail; and a group of 20 current and former IIT students.'[5]

Arundhati was born in 1982 in Allahabad, and Menaka in 1974 in Hyderabad. Both graduated from the prestigious National Law School of India in Bangalore. 'I had two options: I could have become a professional chess player, or I could have made this commitment and become a lawyer. I think I was twenty-one years old when I went to work for him, and it was hilarious. Everyone around me was four times my age, or three times my age,'[6] said Menaka. After studying and practising abroad, Menaka returned to New Delhi. 'My heart is in constitutional law – Indian constitutional law. Most of my practice, the practice I care most deeply about, is constitutional rights.'[7]

It was through this lens that she argued the writ petition, calling Section 377 'arbitrary'[8], one based on the ideas of Victorian morality. In no uncertain terms, she reminded the court that Section 377 discriminates based on the sex of a person's sexual partner, which made it unconstitutional. To back her argument, she cited Article 15 of the constitution, which forbade discrimination on the basis of sex.

'How strongly must we love, knowing we are unconvicted felons under Section 377?'[9] she asked making a passionate case for decriminalizing Section 377 and ensuring the fundamental rights and liberties of the LGBTQ+ community under the Constitution.

Menaka also alluded to the case of Hadiya, a Kerala medical student who had embraced Islam and wanted to marry a Muslim man. In her case, the top court had upheld her fundamental right under the Indian Constitution to choose her partner. This again affirmed that Section 377 was unconstitutional as it criminalized choosing a same-sex partner and in doing so, violated the principle upheld in Hadiya's case, she argued.

In 2012, the judges in the Suresh Kumar Koushal v. Naz Foundation case (which led to the 2013 SC repeal) kept asking the lawyers about the existence of LGBTQ+ persons. Queer rights lawyer Danish Sheikh, who observed the proceedings, wrote about Menaka: '... she told the judges how many lives were going by living under the shadow of this law ... She opened up the space of what it meant to be queer, speaking of the right to love, of the Court's own mandate in protecting individuals, of times when district judges had protected runaway inter-caste lovers from their families. She spoke about the law's specific impact on transgender persons, on how it impeded the promise of full citizenship that NALSA pointed towards ... At one point, ASG Tushar Mehta attempted to interrupt Menaka Guruswamy, prompting Chief Justice Dipak Misra to snap: "Let her speak!" She spoke, and today, we were heard.'[10]

On 6 September 2018, the five-judge Constitutional bench of the Supreme Court unanimously declared the law unconstitutional 'in so far as it criminalises consensual sexual conduct between adults of the same sex'.[11] It was a historic moment for India. The world was seeing it in a new light. Celebrities took to social media to celebrate victory. Karan Johar was one of the first to tweet: 'Historical judgment!!!! So proud today! Decriminalising homosexuality and abolishing #Section377 is a huge thumbs up for humanity and equal rights! The country gets its oxygen back!'.[12]

For Menaka and Arundhati, who were at the forefront of the fight, 'it was both a personal and professional achievement.'[13] At the same time, they came out, telling Fareed Zakaria of CNN that they were a couple.

The fight for LGBTQ+ rights is not over. In April 2023, the Supreme Court began to hear arguments for the Right to Marriage for same-sex couples. The petitioners, Supriyo Chakraborty and Abhay Dange and many others claimed that the non-recognition of same-sex marriage amounts to discrimination that undermines the dignity and self-fulfilment of LGBTQ+ couples. Menaka and Arundhati are among the many lawyers representing these petitioners. They reminded the court that the identified 7–8 per cent of LGBTQ+ persons in the country cannot be ignored or denied the fundamental rights, nearly 15 in all, enjoyed by heterosexual couples such as adoption rights and the right to salaries.

The petitions sought the provision of the Special Marriage Act of 1954 to accommodate same-sex unions by replacing the term 'man and woman' with 'spouse' without disrupting the ambit of personal laws. Following their marriage, they argued, same-sex individuals should have access to joint bank accounts, health insurance, life insurance and all other benefits that come with marriage.

More than thirty-four nations have legalized same-sex marriage since the Netherlands did so in 2000, either via legislation or judicial rulings. Currently, the adoption of children by same-sex couples is authorized in more than fifty nations. If the Supreme Court gives a positive verdict, India too will join their ranks.

The LGBTQ+ Indians await the decision on this case at this moment. After being criminalized since 1860, when Section 377 was codified in the Indian Penal Code, remaining untouched even after Independence, it is about time that the consensual partnerships of same-sex couples are recognized. Urging the Supreme Court for a positive declaration, Arundhati and Menaka might be at the precipice of helping make more history that will redefine the future of queer Indians and bring them dignity.

Grace Banu

The Warrior

'It was in the eighth standard that I began to feel something about me was different. I wasn't like the other boys in my class,' says Grace Banu.[1] Grace's school days were not like that of the other children, weighted as she was by the double pressure of disadvantaged caste and sexuality. But Grace used her own history to change lives, emerging as a voice for those with similar experiences as her. A Dalit and transgender activist and founder of the Trans Rights Now Collective, Grace created history by becoming the first transgender to secure admission to an engineering college in Tamil Nadu. Today, she is at the forefront of the anti-caste and transgender rights movement and is undoubtedly one of the fiercest voices in transgender rights in the country.

Grace was born and raised in Tuticorin district, Tamil Nadu. As a Dalit-transgender person, she dealt with discrimination on a daily basis in her life. She was picked on at school because of her caste and subsequently because of her swiftly developing gender dysphoria. She was not allowed to enter the classroom, had to sit under a tree, far from the other students, and asked to come late to school and leave early. It was made clear to the other students that speaking with her would result in punishment.

The world doubled down on her, and Grace became an alien in that world. She had little access then to announce to the world 'This is gender dysphoria – where you wrestle with your gender identity and the sex-related gender characteristics society has forced on you . . . you will get through this.'[2] Feeling isolated and defeated, she attempted suicide. She was only sixteen at the time.

Banu confessed to her parents that she was a woman and that the male identity thrust on her was a burden. 'My parents weren't [educated] – they didn't know anything about trans persons . . . They thought they'd lost all their dreams, like [their] children have this kind of "problem" – and they put me into an asylum.'[3]

At the asylum, where she was going through conversion therapy to get 'cured' of homosexuality, Grace was introduced to the writings of Dr B.R. Ambedkar and Karl Marx. Dr Ambedkar, who led the crusade against the caste system in India, had a major influence on Grace's understanding of the world around her. She became aware of why she was discriminated against all her childhood.

Her mother, however, did not want her to give up on her education. Every day, we stood outside the principal's office, and my mother begged for my readmission. After several days, they decided to permit me.'[4]

Grace was eventually rejected by her parents in 2008 for her transgender identity. 'I had a tormented childhood ... The people I had around me disappeared the very next day I decided to come out of the closet,' she said of that time.[5] But despite all the challenges, with the support of her trans family and others, Grace finished her diploma in computer science training in 2011 and landed a job in Chennai, working for a software company. Here, too, she faced discrimination and had to leave due to the hostility she faced.

But Grace wasn't ready to give up. She decided to continue with her studies and get into a college. To learn if transgender students were admitted at Anna University, she filed a right to information (RTI) request. They did not, she learnt, but Grace still applied against their guidelines and secured a seat at Sri Krishna College of

Engineering, in Arakkonam, a private college, to study Electrical and Electronics Engineering in 2013.

At barely nineteen, Grace had become the first transgender person to be accepted into a Tamil Nadu engineering institution. But her college journey was not easy. Even though her fees were waived, she was still struggling financially. She had used up all her savings and the money she had borrowed from her friend. Being a transgender, she was unable to find accommodation near her college and had to spend Rs 60 to reach the college.

Hearing about her troubles, Sinthu Govindaswamy, a business consultant for an IT company, launched an online campaign to raise money, and there was considerable response. Grace later completed her diploma and scored 95 per cent. Alongside her education, Grace became an activist and began to fight for transgender rights. She petitioned the Madras High Court, pleading with them to order the Tamil Nadu State Public Commission to permit transgender people to take the admission test. Prithika Yashini was appointed as the nation's first transgender sub-inspector of police as a result of that plea.

The Trans Rights Now Collective Grace founded centres on issues faced by the Dalit caste, Bahujan political party and Adivasi population. She also adopted a daughter, Tharika Banu, who, thanks to her mother, has become the first transgender person to pass the class 12 school-leaving examination in Tamil Nadu. Grace has also fought to get Tharika admitted into the Government Siddha College through Madras High Court, where she had been denied admission. After adopting Tharika, Grace adopted eleven more trans daughters. She swells with pride as she recounts each of their achievements.

The term intersectionality might be new to politics but it explains the struggles and obstacles Grace faced in her life. Because of this term, she also had the rare ability to see transgender issues through the lens of caste. Grace believes that casteism in trans spaces is prevalent and cannot be veiled and that upper-caste transgender personalities dominate leadership positions and get better opportunities. 'What governments need to understand is that the transgender community is not homogenous. Trans people come from various classes, castes, regional, and economic backgrounds. Clubbing them into one homogenous reservation category erases the experiences of Dalit-Adivasi communities. It is unjust,' she said.[6]

Since the NALSA (National Legal Ser. Auth vs Union Of India & Ors on 15 April, 2014) ruling, in which the Supreme Court acknowledged their constitutional rights to equality, liberty and dignity, the transgender community has made the struggle for horizontal reservation a top priority. Grace is a key figure in this fight. Horizontal reservations meant separate reservations for transgenders within each category – Scheduled Castes (SC), Scheduled Tribes (ST), Other Backward Classes (OBC) and the General Category.

In December 2014, Member of Parliament from the DMK Tiruchi Siva proposed a Private Member's Bill seeking horizontal reservation for transgender and intersex persons in education and employment, on the lines of reservation available for women or people with disabilities across caste categories. The Rajya Sabha overwhelmingly approved the measure. However, in 2016, the Transgender Persons (Protection of Rights) Bill 2016 did away with the reservations, resulting in extensive demonstrations spearheaded by the transgender community.

The battle for horizontal reservation has been a protracted one, and transgender persons have been deprived of numerous possibilities because of the delay. Currently, Grace is protesting against being included in the OBC category, a proposed move by the Union Government that amounts to a vertical reservation. This means trans people will face competition from other OBCs for the reserved seat or position, thus decreasing their chances of securing it.

Grace believes that the fairer method would be for the

provision of different reservations inside each vertical, SC/ST/OBC/General category, via horizontal reservations, which will cut across all caste groups. According to a blog post by the Centre for Law and Policy Research, this means that 1 per cent of ST, SC, OBC and general merit seats will each be designated for transgender individuals.

'Karunanidhi [former CM of Tamil Nadu] was one of the first supporters of the trans community. He did a lot for us. But the DMK [Dravida Munnetra Kazhagam] government, which claims to be trans-friendly, is not willing to give us our rights,' Banu told *The Quint.*[7] In 2021, Karnataka became the first and the only Indian state to provide transgender individuals with a 1 per cent horizontal hiring preference for positions in the government service.

In April, Grace took to Twitter to let her stance known on the issue of same-sex marriage, for which the Supreme Court heard numerous petitions filed by same-sex couples. 'Final hearings on #marriageequality before the Supreme Court, all lgbtqia+ persons are happy and eagerly waiting for the victory. Im disappointed as to why don't you people have this much interest in #Horizontalreservationfortrans, this is also our basic right. This is the privilege of your caste, class and power. #EqualityForAll.'[8] Grace articulated how the issue of horizontal reservation for trans people outweighs equal marriage rights for the queer community as a whole, describing the wanting of equal marriage rights arising from caste, class and power-oriented privilege.

When asked how she wants to be remembered, she questioned whether she really will be: 'Our histories, as Dalit people, as trans people, have always been erased. Maybe, in the future, my history will also be erased.'[9] Grace has emerged as a warrior in making this issue known and being a hero to her community. The hope for a better future is only alive because of this kind of fierce activism.

Madhu Bai Kinnar

The Changemaker

On a speeding train from Kolkata to Mumbai you may come across hijras singing, dancing or begging. Madhu was once one of them. She grew up at the crossroads of two marginalized communities, Dalit and transgender, a combination that brought extraordinary pressures upon her. But she leapt over all these challenges to become India's first transgender mayor.

Madhu attended school until the eighth standard, dropping out as a teenager at about fourteen because of the harassment she faced there. Later, she left her home to join the local hijra community. She took the name 'Madhu' – the last name 'Kinnar' derives from her community – and started earning a living by performing odd jobs.

Madhu spent fifteen years busking in trains before she turned to politics. Actually, it was by sheer coincidence that she entered that arena at all. When the local elections of her hometown, Raigarh, in Chhattisgarh were announced, Madhu happened to be in the government offices where they distributed nomination forms. Some elders from her community coaxed her to fill up the sheet. Though she was unsure, she still went ahead. 'I have grown up like a child from the families of this town. They consider me as a member of their families. They felt that if one of their families became the mayor, they would get better public service. They made me contest the election,' she would later say.[1]

Madhu's main motivation, however, was the poor state of Raigarh. 'There were no proper sidewalks. The alleys were dirty and piled high with garbage. Poor people, abandoned in their old age, slept in the streets with nothing to keep them warm. We decided to do something – by running for the coming election,' she said.[2]

It was a tough battle – Madhu had limited funds, and she stood as an independent candidate without the backing of an established party. While many political parties on average can spend up to Rs 70 lakh, she spent about Rs 70,000 from her earnings on her election campaign. But her platform of improving sanitation appealed to the locals disillusioned with the track record of India's two major parties.

On 5 January 2015, she scripted history by winning the mayoral election beating the Bharatiya Janata Party's (BJP) Mahaveer Guru Ji by 4,357 votes. Madhu's win sparked a media sensation. She was sworn in as Raigarh's mayor, wearing a white sari and pink lipstick, with a large red bindi adorning her forehead, and was greeted by cheering supporters who placed marigold garlands around her neck.

'People have shown faith in me,' Madhu told reporters after winning the election. 'I consider this win as the love and blessings of people for me. I'll put in my best efforts to accomplish their dreams. Public support encouraged me to enter the poll fray for the first time, and because of their support only, I emerged as the winner.'[3]

Strictly speaking, Madhu wasn't India's first transgender elected official. In 1999 and again in 2009, transgender women who won local offices reserved for female politicians were disqualified when courts ruled that they were not female. Madhu's win, however, came after nine months when India's Supreme Court legally recognized 'third gender'/transgender persons in the National Legal Services Authority of India (NALSA) judgment (see more on NALSA in the chapter on Laxmi

Narayan Tripathi) and said that third gender persons were entitled to fundamental rights under the Constitution and under international law. The Supreme Court also directed state governments to develop mechanisms to realize the rights of 'third gender'/transgender persons. It was this pathbreaking judgment that allowed her victory to be acknowledged.

'We've been made fun of, bullied and called names because we're nothing more than kinnar to them . . . If we danced somewhere, people thought we were bad luck,' she said.[4] When she entered public office, she anticipated a similar response. 'I was apprehensive at first . . . I had never appeared before such a huge crowd – all those powerful councillors, officers and deputies,' she said of the day.[5] But the new mayor rolled her sleeves and got ready to work.

Immediately following her swearing-in, Madhu began daily inspections of the city's streets, wells, markets and sanitation systems. She and her team would go on rounds every morning, starting as early as 7 a.m., and urge city workers to fix clogged wells, pipes and gutters. She also quickly made a name for herself as a down-to-earth politician, riding to city hall on a borrowed scooter or by rickshaw or by getting a lift from anyone willing to give one. She did, however, have a bodyguard, just in case! Her commitment towards her job and her visibility sparked a change in behaviour across Raigarh, with everyday citizens treating not only her but also her fellow kinnars with more respect. Madhu was now often called mausi (aunty) or didi (sister).

As a result of this hard work, Raigarh won the Swachhata Excellence Award in 2019 – this is how clean the city had become. Madhu's win might have gone unacknowledged in the back-and-forth of politics because of her identity, but her impact was undeniable. Now that she has transcended from being a hijra who begs and busks for a living, her vision for the community is also the same. Madhu wishes to see hijras step into the mainstream and be a prominent part of this world. She appointed Kunti, a hijra, as her assistant as one of the steps to bring the community to light. Always believing in change and putting in the work to bring it about, Madhu Bai Kinnar was born to be a changemaker.

Rituparno Ghosh

A Vision Like No Other

One of the most gifted storytellers in Indian cinema, Rituparno Ghosh was not just a successful filmmaker who heralded a new wave in Bengali cinema and won nineteen National Awards but was also openly transgender. He* constantly challenged societal stereotypes through his films and his personal life. When he went bald or lined his eyes with kohl or dressed flamboyantly, he presented

---

* Rituparno Ghosh lived a dynamic life at a time the complexity of which couldn't be comprehended by many. Their entire life they were referred to by he/him pronouns. When adverting to Ghosh, most sources use he/his/him pronouns, though some have mentioned they were a trans woman and/or genderqueer. Ghosh fiercely transcended the binaries of gender and never confirmed their gender expression. This chapter will use he/him/his pronouns to refer to the filmmaker but will also delve into the nuances of their gender identity.

101

an opportunity for people to question the stereotypes they carried. BBC journalist Amitabha Bhattasali said of him, '. . . through his films, writings and acting roles, Mr Ghosh gave a voice to disempowered sexual minorities. Though mocked by many, he lived life on his own terms and never shied from taking up verbal fights with those who mocked him.'[1]

Born in 1963 in Kolkata, Rituparno spent his early years working in advertising before moving to direction and, in the latter part of his life, into acting. Equipped with a degree in economics from Jadavpur University, Rituparno started working in the media and advertising field as a copywriter. He composed several catchy lines for well-known products and also began to make documentaries. Both these helped him develop sharp precision and detailing in his filmmaking.

It was Rituparno's second film *Unishe April* (19 April) that gave him the real break. Influenced by Satyajit Ray's *Jalshaghar* (*Music Room*), it told the story of an award-winning dancer and her emotionally estranged daughter, who aspires to be a doctor. The film was a hit and even received critical acclaim, garnering two National Film Awards in 1995, including the esteemed Best Feature Film. Two years on, in 1997, Rituparno released *Dahan*, a sensitive film inspired by a true story about sexual molestation, which won three National Film Awards and recognition from various international film festivals.

Other films followed – all of them exploring the sufferings and feelings of women. Many of these won National Film Awards and starred some of the country's most accomplished actors like Kiron Kher, Rakhee, Sharmila Tagore and Nandita Das. In 2003, he made his best-known film, an adaptation of Rabindranath Tagore's novel *Chokher Bali* starring Aishwarya Rai and Raima Sen, which highlighted the sexual desires of widows. The film was another critical and commercial hit, winning three National Film Awards. It was shown in over twenty-five international festivals including the Toronto International Film Festival and was nominated for the Golden Leopard (Best Film) award at the Locarno International Film Festival.

The box-office success of *Chokher Bali* meant that Rituparno could continue to make beautiful, challenging films and also attract mainstream stars like Amitabh Bachchan, Monisha Koirala, Soha Ali Khan, Abhishek Bachchan, Preity Zinta, Arjun Rampal and Ajay Devgan, and music talents like Subha Mugdal and Gulzar Sahab. He also began to make films in Maithili and even English. He won a total of nineteen National Film Awards including two for best film, making him one of the few

Indian filmmakers to get this honour twice. Many of his films were also box office successes in West Bengal.

All through this journey he remained open about his own sexuality. He loved dressing in feminine clothes, wearing makeup and jewellery, and while initially he wore men's clothes, in his final years, he began to dress as a woman almost exclusively. It is said he had a long-term relationship with a married Bengali superstar and only those closest to him knew about it.

Bhattasali said that women loved working with Rituparno since he, of course, would not sexually harass them in any way – in dramatic contrast to the 'casting couch' mentality of many powerful men in Indian cinema. In his autobiographical book, *First Person*, Rituparno openly talked about his personal experiences as a queer personality, the challenges in a male-dominated film industry (Rituparno 'was cautious about sending out the wrong signals to actors,'[2] according to journalist Subhash Jha), and the existing narrative in films from a male lens. He wrote, 'My point is why shouldn't I celebrate my sexuality? . . . There is much more to such relationships. Same-sex relationships, too, are extremely soulful, emotional and have the same pathos that any heterosexual relationship has.'[3]

Despite his own career as an openly queer person,

Rituparno expressed some scepticism about Indian films (or society), treating homosexuality with total honesty or acceptance. He said, 'I don't think *Brokeback Mountain* can be done in Indian cinema. I don't know about our cinema ... the sexual mores, family structures and parameters of the permissible are different.'[4]

In 2011, he belied his own words and acted in two gay- and transgender-themed Bengali films. *Arekti Premer Golpo*, directed by Kaushik Ganguly, was about a transgender documentary filmmaker with a bisexual lover, while *Memories in March* by Sanjoy Nag, told the story of a grieving mother who discovered her son is gay after his death. His performances were so intimate that these two films almost seemed autobiographical.

Rituparno finished his career with the movie *Chitrangada*, an adaptation of Rabindranath Tagore's famous dance drama about Arjuna's wife, the Manipuri princess who dressed and behaved as a man before she met the Pandava prince. Rituparno had a long-standing creative relationship with Tagore's work, but this final film may have been his most personal. Tagore's *Chitrangada* broke the stigmas of gender binary roles when it was written in 1891. Rituparno adapted the character to a contemporary story about a choreographer who struggled with his identity and decided to eventually go through gender reassignment surgery. The story ended with the line 'Be What You Wish to Be'.

Accounts of Rituparno's final years heavily imply that he was transitioning before his death. Dr Rajiv Seal of Fortis Hospitals, his long-standing physician, said that complications had crept up for Rituparno after going through hormone treatments following abdominoplasty and breast implant operations. He had undergone these operations for his role in Kaushik Ganguly's film *Arekti Premer Golpo*. The details of this aspect of his life, however, remain hidden.

For ten years, Rituparno had lived through diabetes mellitus type 2 and in the last five years, he also suffered from pancreatitis. He experienced insomnia and was on medication for it. Then there were the complications from the hormone treatments, according to his doctor. On 30 May 2013, Rituparno died at his Kolkata residence following a massive heart attack. He was only forty-nine.

Rituparno's death triggered tributes from across the Indian film world, as well as from politicians in West Bengal. 'Rituparno Ghosh had a great sense of humour. He had a brilliant understanding of human behaviour. Will miss him and his cinema. RIP my Friend,' tweeted Anupam Kher.[5] A distressed Amitabh Bachchan remarked in a series of tweets: 'A sad day! Rituparno Ghosh, that young and brilliant director producer of some remarkable Bengal films, passes away . . . shocked!![6] Ritu Da, as we affectionately called him, was just 49 . . . he is the only director that has worked with all members of our family!!'[7] Onir, another gay Indian filmmaker, said Rituparno's death marked a big loss for India's LGBTQ+ community as well as for Indian cinema.

The chief minister of West Bengal, Mamata Banerjee, also expressed her condolences: 'We are stunned. In his sudden demise, Bengal has lost an eminent filmmaker. It is a very sad day for us.'[8] The Indian consulate in Bangladesh held a retrospective in Rituparno's remembrance. Mithaq Kazimi, the Afghan-American director, wrote about Rituparno's influence beyond India in his blog and in several newspapers.

Rituparno Ghosh's cinema defied norms of gendered behaviour. Cityspidey, a news platform, said, 'He was probably the first openly queer filmmaker with box office successes who broke cinematic barriers through his subtle depiction of relationships. He strategically aligned himself with the common man's life and established himself as one of them; it made it easy for him to intervene in the private space of people to talk about issues they usually turn a blind eye to, such as alternative sexual identity, gender and subversion of gender roles.'[9] As a person who wore many hats, Rituparno Ghosh will be remembered for many things – his ingenuity in his films and writings, his sensitive portrayal of women and his bold display of his sexuality. But above all, as one of the few mainstream Indian filmmakers who was truly unafraid to explore his sexuality through his work.

Dutee Chand

India's Fastest Woman

Dutee Chand is one of India's top athletes – the sprinter holds the national record in women's 100 metres, and is the first Indian to get a gold in a 100 metres race at a global sporting event. Dutee is also the first openly gay athlete from India. When she announced to her family that she was in a same-sex relationship, Dutee knew that from thereon it would be an uphill road. But she stayed firm, even sharing her partner's photo on social media in 2022.

When Dutee participated in the Queen's P^n alongside Olympic gold medallist diver Tom D ^{to} shed light on homophobia in Commonwealth c ^{ies,} her message was loud and clear. By pushing ^{arj} and showcasing exceptional talent, Dutee h way for thousands of young girls with big dreams, and for greater inclusion and recognition of queer athletes.

Dutee was born in 1996 in Gopalpur, Odisha. Her childhood was spent in poverty. Her father, a weaver, earned as little as ₹200 for a sari he spent over a month weaving. These meagre earnings supported his wife and their five daughters and son. The family lived, ate and slept in one room. But it didn't stop Dutee or her siblings from dreaming big. Her father always backed his daughters to pursue their interest in sports. 'Dutee's talent showed while she was in school. I told her if sports is what you want to do, give it your best shot and she has,' he said.[1]

It was Dutee's elder sister Saraswati Chand who had put the village on the map as a national-level sprinter. She prodded Dutee to become an athlete; it would fetch them government jobs! Dutee took to running, encouraged and guided by her sister. 'When I began running at the age of 0, I didn't have the diet athletes need. It was just rice and etables. Every day,'[2] Dutee said about her childhood tr ng. Despite the lack of resources, Dutee's interest in run kept increasing and she was especially inspired by the g Jamaican runner Usain Bolt and South African middl ance runner Caster Semenya.

The hed moment in Dutee's life came in 2006, at the ag n. That year, Dutee and her sister joined a government sports hostel, taking a significant step towards pursuing their athletic aspirations. Six years on, Duttee had become an under-18 national champion in the 100-metre race. In 2014, she won two gold medals in the Asian Junior Athletics Championships in Taipei and began to prepare for the Commonwealth Games.

However, Dutee's career faced a significant setback that year when she was suspended by the Athletics Federation of India (AFI) due to a controversial gender test. The test revealed that she had hyperandrogenism, a medical condition that results in naturally high levels of testosterone in women.

The AFI's decision sparked a widespread debate about gender and eligibility in sports. The ban was devastating for Dutee. 'I was completely shattered ... My performance deteriorated steadily. I was pushed to third position in the national athletics meet in Bangalore,' she told the BBC.[3]

Her legal team successfully argued the ruling, calling it discriminatory and flawed and took her case to the Court of Arbitration for Sport (CAS). A year on, in 2015, CAS suspended the hyperandrogenism regulations set by the International Association of Athletics Federations, allowing her to compete again. This landmark ruling was not only a personal victory for Dutee but also had broader implications for athletes facing similar challenges worldwide.

Dutee's family felt jubilant that justice had finally prevailed. 'She has endured a lot in that year. Barbs have been aimed at her; she has been called all kinds of names. But now the time has come for her to show the world the stuff she is made of,'[4] a relieved and proud Akhuji Chand, Dutee's mother, said.

'I always believed the ban would be lifted because I knew Dutee was not at fault,' said her sister Saraswati. 'Since the ban, I have been dreading her phone calls. And it was no different on Monday when Dutee called at around ten in the night. I thought, "Here comes another bad news." But the ecstasy in her voice told me this time it was different.'[5]

The ban had been lifted and Dutee didn't want to waste any more time. Putting the trauma behind her, she decided to focus on the upcoming Rio Olympics in 2016. She had to reach the Olympic qualifying mark of 11.32 seconds for the 100 metre event and 23.20 seconds for 200 metres. And she was in a hurry. She knew the ban could be reimposed on her once again. 'It is what God has given me and I know he is with me,' she said.[6] The challenges she faced in the past year had only strengthened her resolve to demonstrate her abilities on the grandest platform of all.

In Hyderabad, Dutee devoted herself to intense training, utilizing her resilience and concentration to surpass the qualifying standards for the 100 and 200 metre races. Despite facing negative comments and scepticism, she maintained her unwavering determination. Her family, neighbours and numerous fans who had witnessed her remarkable journey provided overwhelming support to her during this time.

Dutee went on to qualify for the 2016 Rio Olympics, becoming the first Indian female sprinter to compete at the Olympics in thirty-six years. Although she didn't win a medal, her participation was a historic moment for Indian athletics. In 2018, she won two silver medals at the Asian Games.

The following year, Dutee once again decided to break barriers, but this time, in a different way.

In 2019, at the age of twenty-three, she publicly revealed that she was in a same-sex relationship, making her the first openly queer athlete in India. She said 'coming out of the closet' was better than 'hiding'[7] her personal life from the public and that the Supreme Court verdict of the previous year on Article 377 (for more on 377, read Menaka Guruswamy and Arundhati Katju) had given her the courage to come out.

In interviews, she called her partner her 'soulmate' and said that she wanted to break the silence around same-sex relationships in India and inspire others who faced similar struggles. Dutee Chand's coming out made waves and had a significant impact on the LGBTQ+ community in India and beyond. Equal rights activist Harish Iyer called her a 'beacon of hope'.[8] Talk show host Ellen DeGeneres tweeted, 'She's the 100 m record holder and the first openly gay sportsperson in India. I guess she knows a thing or two about being first. I'm so proud of her.'[9] Shashi Tharoor said, 'Dutee Chand's story is one of remarkable courage against the odds . . . Character and courage triumphing over circumstance – hers is the stuff of legend!'[10]

However, Dutee's coming out also brought its challenges and obstacles. Speaking of the backlash she faced back home, she said, 'it is going to take time for people in my village to get used to the idea.'[11] Her family, too, had not taken well to the news and there was severe pressure on her.

The media attention about her private life left her shaken. She was concerned for her partner who also came from a poor weaving family and had moved to Bhubaneshwar to complete her studies. 'I asked her to move out so that the media attention and village taunts wouldn't disrupt her studies,'[12] Dutee said.

Despite the pressures, she kept her head held high

and remains a role model for the LGBTQ+ community. During the opening ceremony of the 2022 Commonwealth Games in Birmingham, Dutee unfurled the Pride flag, sending out a powerful message to the world.

During the Games, Tom Daley shared a photo on Twitter featuring seven LGBTQ+ athletes and activists from various countries. Their act of unfurling the Pride flag aimed to draw attention to the unfortunate reality that homosexuality remains criminalized in more than half of the Commonwealth countries. Shockingly, in three of these nations, the harshest punishment for being homosexual is death.

Dutee Chand joined chorus with Daley in demanding the right for queer athletes to feel safe and comfortable without the threat of prosecution or death. Later, she received an invitation from the Commonwealth Games 2022 officials to be the brand ambassador and join Daley.

Dutee continues to compete at both national and international levels, and remains a vocal champion of LGBTQ+ rights. As the fight for the legal recognition of same-sex marriage in India intensified, she said, 'several countries have granted recognition to same-sex marriages. This should happen in India too.'[13] Dutee has received many awards, including India's second highest sporting award, the Arjuna Award, in 2021. Her story serves as a reminder that no dream is too big and no obstacle insurmountable.

Reshma

Kashmir's Trans Icon

Reshma was a well-known singer and transgender activist in Kashmir, whose music videos received a million views on social media. War-torn Kashmir has had a poor record of transgender rights, partly because of the militancy and also religious dogma, and Reshma was the first transgender person to become a leader and voice for the community in the region.

Reshma was born in 1950 in Srinagar into a family of seven children. By the time she was eleven, she had found her talent and love for singing and dancing. 'Every time I heard a Kashmiri song in the background, I would sing and dance along. My family took umbrage at my changing behaviour. They thrashed me many times but I was defiant and adamant. If only they knew of my inner conflicts.'[1]

As a child, she was bullied for her feminine clothing choices and style of speaking. She dropped out of school around the age of thirteen after class five and began working as a tailor under the supervision of her uncle. 'I would see children my age playing hopscotch and laughing. How could I join them? I knew they would find me strange and poke fun at me,' she said.[2]

Despite the sadness that came her way, Reshma's love for music kept her going. Once, when she was twenty-two, Reshma went to a client's home in the posh Lal Bazar locality to drop off some clothes. '. . . I got into a conversation with the family; their daughter insisted that I sing a song. The family acknowledged my talent and showered praise,' Reshma said.[3] A male member of the family then nicknamed her 'Reshma', which was to become her public name years later.

When a thrilled Reshma returned home that day and narrated the incident, expressing her wish to pursue singing, her mother burst into tears. She felt the family had ridiculed her child and she forbade Reshma from singing again. So Reshma decided not to pursue singing – and held back both her songs and her dreams.

Two decades on, she finally found her voice again. In 2001, when she was in her early forties, Reshma began taking care of her brother's four children after he died in an accident. Her decision created an uproar in her family. 'How can a transgender [person] raise a family? This question was continuously posed to me,' she said.[4] But she held still. She also realized the money that she was making from tailoring wouldn't suffice to support her new extended family. That is when she decided to start singing at weddings.

The singing took off. The guests noticed her at gatherings because of her androgynous and vivid persona. Soon she was being invited to every other gathering and wedding in Srinagar. Reshma had a unique voice for singing. She used the popular folk drum of Kashmir called the tumbaknaer as her musical accompaniment. Her melodies were full of charm, and her songs of love and heartbreak were infused with folklore and raunchy laughter. In her recitals, she would often criticize a lover's behaviour towards their beloved in a colourful manner, frequently interspersing her singing with a 'Hai Hai'.

So popular was she that Reshma started receiving invitations from Kashmiri Pandits to perform at their weddings too. Soon she was taking part in concerts throughout Kashmir and across the country. Her most popular song, 'Hai Hai Wesyee', catapulted her to celebrity status after a video of the performance went viral on social media in 2018, and it has since been viewed over 1.4 million times on social media.

For Aijaz Bund, a Kashmir scholar, LGBTQ+ activist and the author of *Hijras of Kashmir: A Marginalized Form of Personhood*, which was the first ethnographic account of the transgenders of Kashmir, Reshma was a person who fought against the stigma faced by the transgender community and also one who made a name for herself as a singer, which was an achievement in itself.

Amid this fame, Reshma continued 'matchmaking' – a traditional profession for the transgender community in the Valley to earn livelihoods as Kashmiris consider them born for it. The job of matchmaking gave her immense respect among the locals. But with time this profession got diluted because of virtual platforms entering into the arena.

Like most of India, transgenders, also known as 'Khwaja-sira' (a member of a traditional transgender third-gender in Pakistan and India since the Mughal times) in Kashmir, are heavily discriminated against in the state. But there is an additional factor. Kashmir has been a conflict zone in some form for at least three decades. 'The decades-old conflict has overshadowed their plight and recent advances in trans rights have done little to improve their conditions,' said Aijaz Bund.[5]

In spite of the Transgender Persons (Protection of Rights) Act passed in 2019 (see more on NALSA in the chapter on Laxmi Narayan Tripathi), the implementation and awareness of these laws are limited and many transgender people struggle every day to even prove their identity to the authorities in the Kashmir Valley. They lack avenues for earning a living, with matchmaking and singing at weddings regarded as their traditional professions. Many have a hard time claiming property rights and are thrown out of their families.

Reshma was often spat on and physically harassed by strangers, not paid by customers and beaten when she demanded payment, and once even forced by some security personnel in Kashmir to sing and dance, which caused her deep humiliation. When a video of her reciting verses from the Quran took the internet by storm, she was made to apologize in a humiliating way by a cleric who issued a decree and asked her to shut down her activism. She also received immense abuse on social media. 'It took a strong toll on my mind, and I was confined to my house for many days,' Reshma said.[6]

Nonetheless, she continued to be at the forefront of the transgender community's struggle for dignity in Kashmir. She frequently visited Hazratbal mosque, where she planned meet-ups with the local transgender population, and the mosque quickly became the epicentre of the Valley's transgender movement. In her talks, she would encourage the community to get an education and find professional jobs like transgender people did in many parts of the world.

But Reshma did not stay away from commenting on state politics. Alongside Aijaz Bund, she continued to fight the government to rehabilitate her own people. Bund had filed a PIL in the Srinagar High Court in 2017 seeking greater inclusion for the community but it went nowhere. Finally after their joint efforts, The Integrated Social Security Scheme (ISSS) for the transgender community was launched by the J&K administrative council in 2020. But despite the legislation, the community continued to face challenges – for example, not having any identity card, which they would need to be accepted into the scheme as many had run away from home without their documentation. Reshma was instrumental in helping transgenders around the Valley recover their documents from their ancestral homes.

Then came another turning point in Reshma's life,

which turned out to be both daunting and liberating. When the whole world was forced to stay indoors due to the COVID-19 pandemic, one of Reshma's songs crossed 5.2 million views, where she was featured alongside Sanam Basit, a new-age Kashmiri folk singer. She was then struggling financially as people had closed their doors on them. 'As marriages were cancelled and people's movements were restricted, match-making took a hit. Many of my colleagues had a family to support especially aged parents,' Reshma said.[7]

She received more fame two years on, in 2022, when she was featured in a documentary on transgender Kashmiri people titled *Trans Kashmir*. The documentary delved into her life and the lives of other Kashmiri transgenders and highlighted the difficulties they faced. That same year Reshma was diagnosed with gastric cancer.

Within months of the diagnosis, Reshma passed away in November 2022 at the age of 70, leaving behind a lasting legacy through her songs and tireless work for the transgender community. The region was filled with grief following her passing. Her long-time collaborator Aijaz Bund said, 'I lost my support system. I am still not able to reconcile that Reshma is no more.'[8]

Transgenders from the state gathered for her funeral. Khushi, a nineteen-year-old transperson, expressed the collective grief perfectly: 'Wo ek aisa Chinar thay, jinhone apni jadein poore Kashmir mein phailayi thi (They were like a Chinar tree, which has its roots spread across Kashmir).'[9]

Notes and Sources

Pawan Dhall, Owais Khan and Rafique-Ul-Haque-Dowjah-Ranjan

1. Sandip Roy, 'Friendship Walk '99: Revisiting India's First Pride March in Kolkata on Its 20th Anniversary', Firstpost, 29 June 2019, https://www.firstpost.com/living/friendship-99-revisiting-indias-first-pride-march-in-kolkata-on-its-20th-anniversary-6898311.html.
2. Ibid.
3. 'A Walk to Remember', *Gaylaxy*, 15 July 2010, https://www.gaylaxymag.com/exclusive/a-walk-to-remember/.
4. According to the report titled 'World Health Organization International Classification of Diseases-10, 2006' "'men who have sex with men (MSM)" refers to any man who has sex with a man, thus accommodating a variety of sexual identities as well as those who do not self-identify as homosexual or gay.' The term, coined by epidemiologists in the 1990s to study the spread of diseases like HIV in this group and subsequently used in medical and social research, refers to sexual behaviour and not sexual orientation.

5. 'A Walk to Remember', *Gaylaxy*, 15 July 2010, https://www.gaylaxymag.com/exclusive/a-walk-to-remember/.

6. Ibid.

7. Sandip Roy, 'Friendship Walk '99: Revisiting India's First Pride March in Kolkata on Its 20th Anniversary', Firstpost, 29 June 2019, https://www.firstpost.com/living/friendship-99-revisiting-indias-first-pride-march-in-kolkata-on-its-20th-anniversary-6898311.html.

8. 'A Walk to Remember', *Gaylaxy*, 15 July 2010, https://www.gaylaxymag.com/exclusive/a-walk-to-remember/.

9. Sandip Roy, 'Friendship Walk '99: Revisiting India's First Pride March in Kolkata on Its 20th Anniversary', Firstpost, 29 June 2019, https://www.firstpost.com/living/friendship-99-revisiting-indias-first-pride-march-in-kolkata-on-its-20th-anniversary-6898311.html.

10. Ibid.

11. 'A Walk to Remember', *Gaylaxy*, 15 July 2010, https://www.gaylaxymag.com/exclusive/a-walk-to-remember/.

12. Sandip Roy, 'Friendship Walk '99: Revisiting India's First Pride March in Kolkata on Its 20th Anniversary', Firstpost, 29 June 2019, https://www.firstpost.com/living/friendship-99-revisiting-indias-first-pride-march-in-kolkata-on-its-20th-anniversary-6898311.html.

13. Ibid.

14. Ibid.

15. 'A Walk to Remember', *Gaylaxy*, 15 July 2010, https://www.gaylaxymag.com/exclusive/a-walk-to-remember/.

16. Ibid.

17. Sandip Roy, 'Friendship Walk '99: Revisiting India's First Pride March in Kolkata on Its 20th Anniversary', Firstpost, 29 June 2019, https://www.firstpost.com/living/friendship-99-revisiting-indias-first-pride-march-in-kolkata-on-its-20th-anniversary-6898311.html.

Additional Sources

Friendship Walk 20th Anniversary, n.d., https://friendshipwalk20.wordpress.com/.

Anjali Gopalan

1. Poorva Misra-Miller, 'Changing a Billion Minds, twice – Activist Anjali Gopalan and the Fight for LGBTQIA+ Rights in India', *Brown Girl Magazine*, 20 August 2021, https://browngirlmagazine.com/changing-a-billion-minds-twice-activist-anjali-gopalan-and-the-fight-for-lgbtqia-rights-in-india/.
2. See note 4 in chapter 1 (Pawan Dhall, Owais Khan and Rafique-Ul-Haque-Dowjah-Ranjan).
3 Suketu Mehta, 'Anjali Gopalan', *Time*, 18 April 2012, https://content.time.com/time/specials/packages/article/0,28804,2111975_2111976_2112141,00.html.
4. Poorva Misra-Miller, 'Changing a Billion Minds, twice – Activist Anjali Gopalan and the Fight for LGBTQIA+ Rights in India', *Brown Girl Magazine*, 20 August 2021, https://browngirlmagazine.com/changing-a-billion-minds-twice-activist-anjali-gopalan-and-the-fight-for-lgbtqia-rights-in-india/.

5. '377. Unnatural Offences', Indian Kanoon, https://indiankanoon.org/doc/1569253/.

6. Kian Ganz, 'The Lawyer Who Fought the 377 Law and Won: Anand Grover', Legally India, 17 August 2009, https://www.legallyindia.com/content/anand-grover-the-lawyer-who-fought-the-377-law-and-won-20090817-134.

7. 'Naz Foundation v. Govt. of NCT of Delhi', Wikipedia, 19 April 2023, https://en.wikipedia.org/wiki/Naz_Foundation_v._Govt._of_NCT_of_Delhi.

8. Sangeeta Barooah Pisharoty, 'Popular and Personal', *The Hindu*, 20 December 2013, https://www.thehindu.com/features/metroplus/society/popular-and-personal/article5483312.ece.

9. Ibid.

Additional Sources

Suneera Tandon, 'Here Are the Crusaders Who've Spent Decades Fighting for Gay Rights in India', Quartz, 6 September 2018, https://qz.com/india/1379618/section-377-indias-crusaders-who-stood-up-for-gay-rights.

Aparna Kalra, 'Anand Grover & Othrs. Vs Prejudice', *Business Standard*, 4 Feb 2014, https://www.business-standard.com/article/current-affairs/anand-grover-othrs-vs-prejudice-114011100499_1.html.

Anoo Bhuyan, 'Documenting Anand Grover, Indira Jaising's Fight for Human Rights Over the Years', The Wire, 20 June 2019, https://thewire.in/law/documenting-anand-grover-india-jaisings-fight-for-human-rights-over-the-years.

Anoo Bhuyan, 'As SC Begins Hearing Challenge to Section 377, a Look at the Law's Journey So Far', The Wire, 10 July 2018, https://thewire.in/law/as-sc-begins-hearing-challenge-to-section-377-a-look-at-the-laws-journey-so-far.

Kian Ganz, 'The Lawyer Who Fought the 377 Law and Won: Anand Grover', Legally India, 17 August 2009, https://www.legallyindia.com/content/anand-grover-the-lawyer-who-fought-the-377-law-and-won-20090817-134.

'Shri. Chevalier, Anjali Gopalan', Srishti Madurai (accessed via Internet Archive), 2015, https://web.archive.org/web/20150302201753/http://srishtiglobal.org/main/node/99.

Suketu Mehta, 'The World's 100 Most Influential People: 2012', Time, 18 April, 2012, https://content.time.com/time/specials/packages/article/0,28804,2111975_2111976_2112141,00.html.

Anoo Bhuyan, '"Now or Later, It Has to Happen" – Anjali Gopalan on Civil Rights for LGBTQs', The Wire, 12 July 2018, https://thewire.in/lgbtqia/watch-anjali-gopalan-on-17-years-of-fighting-against-section-377.

Dhairya Maheshwari, 'Anjali Gopalan: "We're One of the Most Depraved Societies in the World"', National Herald, 19 August 2018, https://www.nationalheraldindia.com/interview/we-are-one-of-the-most-depraved-societies-in-the-world-anjali-gopalan.

Kunal Chauhan, 'Stereotypes and Social Transformation: A Conversation with Anjali Gopalan', Dhaara, 19 November 2020, https://dhaaramagazine.in/2020/11/19/stereotypes-

and-social-transformation-a-conversation-with-anjali-gopalan/.

Dhamini Ratnam, 'We Need to Engage with Whoever is in Power: Anjali Gopalan', *Mint*, 23 May 2014, https://www.livemint.com/Politics/dTB5iuLa53jTVyFYgVMFJL/No-matter-who-is-in-power-we-need-to-continue-to-engage-An.html.

Ashok Row Kavi

1. 'Project Bolo: Ashok Row Kavi', The Humsafar Trust, Solaris Pictures and UNDP India, 17 September 2011, https://www.youtube.com/watch?v=6xFCj-peZmA.

2 Ibid.

3. Ibid.

4. Ibid.

5 Ibid.

6 Ashok Row Kavi, 'The Contract of Silence', in *Yaarana: Gay Writing from South Asia*, ed., Hoshang Merchant, Penguin India, 2010.

7. Ibid.

8. Ibid.

9. Nonita Kalra, 'Ashok Row Kavi: The Real Maha Maharani', *Man's World*, 04 June 2000, https://www.mansworldindia.com/currentedition/from-the-magazine/ashok-row-kavi-real-maha-maharani/.

10. Ibid.

11. Aparnna Hajirnis, 'Ashok Row Kavi: The Pioneering Gay Activist Who Has Seen the Worst and Best Of Times', *Man's World*, 22 March 2022, https://www.mansworldindia.

com/currentedition/mw-anniversary-special-indias-first-gay-rights-activist-looks-back/.

12. Nonita Kalra, 'Ashok Row Kavi: The Real Maha Maharani', *Man's World*, 04 June 2000, https://www.mansworldindia. com/currentedition/from-the-magazine/ashok-row-kavi-real-maha-maharani/.

13. Ridhima Gupta Gupta, '"Don't Need To Dissociate Myself From My Religion To Be A Gay," One Of India's First Gay Rights Activists', thelogicalIndian.com, 24 September 2018, https://thelogicalindian.com/exclusive/ashok-row-kavi/

Additional Sources

'An Interview with Ashok Row Kavi – Coming Out in India', amfAR (accessed via the Internet Archive), 2014, https:// web.archive.org/web/20140725234106/http://amfar.org/ articles/around-the-world/treatasia/older/an-interview-with-ashok-row-kavi%E2%80%94coming-out-in-india/.

'About Us', The Humsafar Trust, https://humsafar.org/about-us/.

Nandita Singh and Nikhil Rampal, 'India's first and oldest gay rights activist is also on the extreme right of RSS', *ThePrint*, 21 July 2018, https://theprint.in/politics/indias-first-and-oldest-gay-activist-uses-a-brand-of-hindutva-to-fight-377/85919/.

Vikram Phukan, 'Bombay Dost, India's first LGBT magazine, turns 25!', *Mid-day*, 6 October 2015, https://www.mid-day. com/mumbai/mumbai-news/article/bombay-dost--india-s-first-lgbt-magazine--turns-25--16587189.

'Ashok Row Kavi: Indian Gay Pioneer and Journalist', lgbthistorymonth.com, https://lgbthistorymonth.com/ashok-row-kavi?tab=biography.

Lisa, 'Gay Leader Ashok Row Kavi Interview With Out & Around', Global Gayz, 9 January 2012, https://www.globalgayz.com/gay-leader-ashok-row-kavi-interview-with-out-around/1898/.

Samanth Subramanian, 'For a lot of people, it's already too late', *Mint*, 17 September 2009, https://www.livemint.com/Politics/priZWzjeGEvhW7EBfXg3gN/8216For-a-lot-of-people-it8217s-already-too-late821.html.

Shuriah Niazi, 'India's First HIV Treatment Centre and Clinic for the LGBTQ', Fairplanet, 15 May 2019, https://www.fairplanet.org/story/indias-first-hiv-treatment-centre-and-clinic-for-the-lgbtq/.

Wikipedia Contributors, 'Ashok Row Kavi', Wikipedia, 6 May 2023, https://en.wikipedia.org/w/index.php?title=Ashok_Row_Kavi&oldid=1153491287.

Laxmi Narayan Tripathi

1. Salman Rushdie, *Languages of Truth: Essays 2003–2020*, Penguin, 2021.
2. The Hindi translation would be 'I'm coming' or 'I'm on my way'. But instead of saying 'aata', the masculine form of the verb 'aana', Laxmi would use the feminine form 'aati'.
3. 'The Red Lipstick Monologue: Laxmi Speaks Her Mind in Her New Book', *Hindustan Times*, 20 August 2016, https://www.hindustantimes.com/the-red-lipstick-monologue-laxmi-speaks-her-mind-in-this-excerpt-from-her-new-book/story-tBWYW6EyocFGGQ6vMSOzlI.html.

4. 'Project Bolo: Laxmi Narayan Tripathi', The Humsafar Trust, Solaris Pictures and UNDP India, YouTube, 17 September 2011, https://www.youtube.com/watch?v=eEW_OCpNL3k.

5. For instance, Laxmi Narayan Tripathi invokes this line in her interview with Barkha Dutt (Lax: Good Girls Go To Heaven And Bad Girls Go Everywhere', Women in the World, YouTube, 8 April 2017, https://www.youtube.com/watch?v=bi6U8FCY_UM) and in her interview to *Guernica* magazine (Shanoor Seervai, 'Laxmi Narayan Tripathi: India's Third Gender', *Guernica*, 16 March 2015, https://www.guernicamag.com/indias-third-gender/).

6. Saba Shabbir, 'Review: Larger than life: Me Hijra, Me Laxmi By Laxmi Tripathi', *Dawn*, 4 October 2015, https://www.dawn.com/news/1210459/review-larger-than-life-me-hijra-me-laxmi-by-laxmi-tripathi.

7. Laxmi Narayan Tripathi, *Red Lipstick: The Men in My Life*, Penguin, 2016.

8. Laxmi Narayan Tripathi, *Me Hijra, Me Laxmi*, Oxford University Press, 2015, p. 43.

9. Ibid., p. 47.

10 Preeti Mehra, 'A Free Country, Again', *Business Line*, 25 April 2014, https://www.thehindubusinessline.com/blink/meet/A-free-country-again/article20759122.ece.

11. Laxmi Narayan Tripathi, *Me Hijra, Me Laxmi*, Oxford University Press, 2015, p. 123.

12. Rajiv Nayan Chaturvedi, 'Our Aim Is To Regain The Lost Space Of Transgender Community In Hindu Religion: Laxmi Narayan Tripathi', *Outlook*, 20 April 2022, https://

www.outlookindia.com/culture-society/eunuchs-have-sacred-place-in-sanatan-dharma-we-are-fighting-to-regain-it-says-trans-activist-laxmi-narayan-tripathi-news-192284.

13. Laxmi Narayan Tripathi, *Me Hijra, Me Laxmi*, Oxford University Press, 2015, pp. 62–63.

14. Laxmi Narayan Tripathi, *Red Lipstick: The Men in My Life*, Penguin, 2016.

15 'National Legal Services Authority v. Union of India', Wikipedia, 29 June 2023, https://en.wikipedia.org/wiki/National_Legal_Services_Authority_v._Union_of_India.

16. Saba Shabbir, 'REVIEW: Larger than life: Me Hijra, Me Laxmi By Laxmi Tripathi', *Dawn*, 4 October 2015.

17. Ibid.

18. Nick Francis, Claudine Spera, Liz Ford, Jessica Edwards, Speakit Films, 'Being Laxmi: "I Belong to the Hijra, the Oldest Transgender Community" – Video', *The Guardian*, 3 September 2015, https://www.theguardian.com/global-development/video/2015/sep/03/being-laxmi-narayan-tripathi-hijra-india-transgender-community-video.

Additional Sources:

Upasana Kamineni Konidela, 'A Conversation With Laxmi Narayan Tripathi: India's Most Prominent Transgender Rights Activist', UR Life [YouTube], 3 December 2021, https://ur.life/article/a-conversation-with-laxmi-narayan-tripathi-indias-most-prominent-transgender-rights-leader.

Bhupen Khakhar

1. 'Bhupen Khakhar: 1934–2003', The Art of India 2023, https://theartofindia.in/collections/bhupen-khakhar.

2. 'Howard Hodgkin & Shanay Jhaveri: Memories of an Indian Master', Indian & South Asian Modern & Contemporary Art, Sotheby's, 12 October 2017, https://www.sothebys.com/en/articles/howard-hodgkin-shanay-jhaveri-memories-of-an-indian-master.

3. 'Bhupen Khakhar', Artforum, December 2016, https://www.artforum.com/print/201610/bhupen-khakhar-64802.

4. 'Smashing India's Sexual Taboos', BBC News, 29 October 2002, http://news.bbc.co.uk/2/hi/entertainment/2372697.stm.

5. 'Bhupen Khakhar, 4 Figures', saffronart.com, https://www.saffronart.com/fixed/ItemDetails.aspx?iid=9222&ampa=BhupenKhakhar.

6. Timothy Hyman RA, 'Bhupen Khakhar's Courageous Work, "Two Men In Benares"', Sotheby's, 3 June 2019, https://www.sothebys.com/en/articles/bhupen-khakhars-courageous-work-two-men-in-benares-1982.

7. 'Smashing India's Sexual Taboos', BBC News, 29 October 2002, http://news.bbc.co.uk/2/hi/entertainment/2372697.stm.

Additional Sources

Amit Chaudhuri, 'Bombay Dreams: How Painter Bhupen Khakhar Captured the City Spirit', *The Guardian*, 21 May

2016, https://www.theguardian.com/artanddesign/2016/may/21/bombay-dreams-how-bhupen-khakahar-captured-spirit-of-city.

'Bhupen Khakhar / His Figurative Paintings Directed to Whole Humanity', Sunpride, 21 February 2023, http://sunpride.hk/bhupen-khakhar-figurative-paintings-directed-whole-humanity/.

Bhupen Khakhar', culturebase.net (accessed via the Internet Archive), 2004, https://web.archive.org/web/20070205125128/http://www.culturebase.net/a'rtist.php?834.

'Bhupen Khakhar', Artiana, http://bhupen-khakhar.com/.

Saurav Bhanot, 'Bhupen Khakhar's Iconic Gay Painting Sets a Record by Being Sold for Rs 22 Crore', *GQ India*, 12 June 2019, https://www.gqindia.com/get-smart/content/bhupen-khakhar-gay-painting-two-men-in-benares-set-a-record-by-being-sold-for-rs-22-crore-auctioned-at-sothebys-in-london.

Balraj Sohal, '5 Top Paintings by Indian Artist Bhupen Khakhar', Desiblitz, 23 November 2021, https://www.desiblitz.com/content/5-top-paintings-by-indian-artist-bhupen-khakhar.

Holland Cotter, 'Bhupen Khakhar, 69, Painter; Influenced a Generation in India', *The New York Times*, 18 August 2003, https://www.nytimes.com/2003/08/18/arts/bhupen-khakhar-69-painter-influenced-a-generation-in-india.html.

Saleem Kidwai and Ruth Vanita

1. Suzanne Goldenberg, 'Saleem Kidwai, Scholar Who Unearthed Long-Buried Literature on Gay Love in India, Dies at 70', *The Washington Post*, 2 September 2021, https://www.washingtonpost.com/local/obituaries/saleem-kidwai-dead/2021/09/02/662ec93c-0a90-11ec-aea1-42a8138f132a_story.html.

2. Ruth Vanita and Saleem Kidwai (eds.), *Same-Sex Love in India*, Palgrave-Macmillan, 2001, p. 56.

3. Ibid.

4. Ibid., p. 108.

5. Ibid., p. 124.

6. Ibid.

7. Ibid., p. 191.

8. Ibid.

9. Ibid.

10. Ibid., p. 196.

11. Suzanne Goldenberg, 'Saleem Kidwai, Scholar Who Unearthed Long-Buried Literature on Gay Love in India, Dies at 70', *The Washington Post*, 2 September 2021, https://www.washingtonpost.com/local/obituaries/saleem-kidwai-dead/2021/09/02/662ec93c-0a90-11ec-aea1-42a8138f132a_story.html.

12. Hoshang Merchant and Akshaya K. Rath, *Gay Icons of India*, Pan Macmillan, 2019.

13. Akhil Katyal, 'Review: The Broken Rainbow by Ruth Vanita', *Hindustan Times*, 27 May 2023, https://www.hindustantimes.com/books/ruth-vanita-s-the-broken-

rainbow-a-testament-to-the-confluence-of-the-academic-and-affective-in-poetry-and-history-101685110253944.html.

14. Suzanne Goldenberg, 'Saleem Kidwai, Scholar Who Unearthed Long-Buried Literature on Gay Love in India, Dies at 70', *The Washington Post*, 2 September 2021, https://www.washingtonpost.com/local/obituaries/saleem-kidwai-dead/2021/09/02/662ec93c-0a90-11ec-aea1-42a8138f132a_story.html.

15. '14961_2016_Judgement_06-Sep-2018.pdf', Sci.gov.in, 2018. p.13 note 6, https://main.sci.gov.in/supremecourt/2016/14961/14961_2016_Judgement_06-Sep-2018.pdf.

16. Sunil Gupta, 'To Saleem Kidwai: A Letter to a Friendship', *Hindustan Times*, 30 August 2021, https://www.hindustantimes.com/opinion/to-saleem-kidwai-a-letter-to-a-friendship-101630338764308.html.

Additional Sources

Shohini Ghosh, 'For Saleem Kidwai, a Politics of Resistance Was Impossible Without Pleasure', *The Wire*, 5 September 2021, https://thewire.in/history/for-saleem-kidwai-a-politics-of-resistance-was-impossible-without-pleasure.

Mario da Penha, 'Saleem Kidwai Stood Against the Tide, in Life and Work', *Mint*, 2 September 2021, https://lifestyle.livemint.com/news/big-story/saleem-kidwai-stood-against-the-tide-in-life-and-work-111630500986982.html.

Sharif D. Rangnekar, 'A Tribute to Saleem Kidwai, a Man Who Made a Real Contribution to India's LGBTQ Community', *Hindustan Times*, 3 September 2021, https://www.hindustantimes.com/books/a-tribute-to-saleem-kidwai-a-man-who-made-a-real-contribution-to-indias-lgbtq-community-101630576812737.html.

Mehru Jaffer, 'Farewell, Saleem Kidwai', *Hindustan Times*, 30 August 2021, https://www.hindustantimes.com/books/farewell-saleem-kidwai-101630332364000.html.

Solaris Pictures, 'Project Bolo – Salim Kidwai', YouTube, 6 November 2011, https://www.youtube.com/watch?v=sEm38vCa0MY.

R. Raj Rao, 'Saleem Kidwai (1951–2021): A Pioneering Historian of Same-Sex Love in India', *Scroll.in*, 31 August 2021, https://scroll.in/article/1004201/saleem-kidwai-1951-2021-a-pioneering-historian-of-same-sex-love-in-india.

Gautam Bhan, 'Ruth Vanita and Saleem Kidwai in Conversation', *Wasafiri* 22 (1)30 January 2007, pp. 52–56.

Wendell Rodricks

1. Debarati S. Sen, ' Wendell Rodricks: Being a Homosexual in the 70s–80s Was Sheer Cold Terror', *The Times of India*, (indiatimes.com), 13 February 2020, https://timesofindia.indiatimes.com/city/mumbai/wendell-rodricks-being-a-homosexual-in-the-70s-80s-was-sheer-cold-terror/articleshow/74113144.cms.

2. Sandip Roy, 'Wendell Rodricks Was an Icon of Indian's LGBTQ Rights Movement – A Pioneer Who Ventured

Where Few Had Dared To', Firstpost, 15 February 2020, https://www.firstpost.com/living/wendell-rodricks-was-an-icon-of-indians-lgbtq-rights-movement-a-pioneer-who-ventured-where-few-had-dared-to-8041731.html.

3. Ibid.

4. Ibid.

5. Debarati S. Sen, 'Wendell Rodricks: Being a Homosexual in the 70s–80s Was Sheer Cold Terror', *The Times of India*, (indiatimes.com), 13 February 2020.

6. Premankur Biswas, 'How Wendell Rodricks Taught a Generation of Indian Gay Men to Be Comfortable in Their Skin', *The Indian Express*, 13 February 2020, https://indianexpress.com/article/opinion/web-edits/wendell-rodricks-homosexuality-india-gay-rights-6266411/.

7. Sandip Roy, 'Wendell Rodricks Was an Icon of Indian's LGBTQ Rights Movement – A Pioneer Who Ventured Where Few Had Dared To', Firstpost, 15 February 2020, https://www.firstpost.com/living/wendell-rodricks-was-an-icon-of-indians-lgbtq-rights-movement-a-pioneer-who-ventured-where-few-had-dared-to-8041731.html.

8 'The Insider', *Pune Mirror*, 26 August 2012, https://punemirror.com/entertainment/bollywood/the-insider/cid5135487.htm.

9. Wendell Rodricks, 'How Wendell Rodricks Started His Fashion Boutique in GOA, Well Before Designers Had Their Own Shops', Scroll, 13 February 2020, , https://scroll.in/article/952973/how-wendell-rodricks-started-his-fashion-boutique-in-goa-well-before-designers-had-their-own-shops.

10. Shweta Shiware, '11 Moments That Made Wendell Rodricks a Top Influencer', *Mid-Day*, 20 February 2020, https://www.mid-day.com/mumbai/mumbai-news/article/11-moments-that-made-Wendell-Rodricks-a-top-influencer-22633227.

11. Dhamini Ratnam, 'Designer, Activist, Writer: Wendell Rodricks Wore Many Hats', *Hindustan Times*, 13 February 2020, https://www.hindustantimes.com/india-news/designer-activist-writer-wendell-rodricks-wore-many-hats/story-yYwrwo9g9lv0yBPoO9KmLO.html.

12. Chintan Girish Modi, 'Masaba Gupta Pays Tribute to Wendell Rodricks in Season 2 of Masaba Masaba', Firstpost, 5 August 2022, https://www.firstpost.com/art-and-culture/masaba-gupta-pays-tribute-to-wendell-rodricks-in-season-2-of-masaba-masaba-11016671.html.

Additional Sources

Saumya Sharma, 'Wendell Rodricks Envisioned Fashion as a Tool for Empowerment', *Hindustan Times*, 13 February 2020, https://www.hindustantimes.com/lifestyle/wendell-rodricks-envisioned-fashion-as-a-tool-for-empowerment/story-9RLa96mT6m4n4nHhd56lGO.html.

Shrishti Negi, 'Wendell Rodricks Only One Who Supported LGBTQ Community, Says India's First Plus Size Queer Model', News18, 13 February 2020, https://www.news18.com/news/lifestyle/wendell-rodricks-only-one-who-supported-lgbtq-community-says-indias-first-plus-size-queer-model-2499031.html.

'Wendell Rodricks: How to Make Your Dreams a Reality', TED Talk, https://www.ted.com/talks/wendell_rodricks_ how_to_make_your_dreams_a_reality/details.

Namrata Zakaria, 'A Beloved Designer, Author & Activist', *Mumbai Mirror*, 13 February 2020, mumbaimirror. indiatimes.com/mumbai/cover-story/a-beloved-designer- author-activist/articleshow/74108677.cms?utm_ source=contentofinterest&utm_medium=text&utm_ campaign=cppst.

Sumana Mukherjee, 'Book Review: The Green Room', *Forbes India*, 6 October 2012, https://www.forbesindia.com/ article/appraisals/book-review-the-green-room/33855/1.

'Excerpts from Wendell Rodricks' The Green Room', 12 October 2012, *The Times of India*(indiatimes.com), https:// timesofindia.indiatimes.com/life-style/books/features/ Excerpts-from-Wendell-Rodricks-The-Green-Room/ articleshow/15746446.cms.

Madhusree Chatterjee/IANS, '20 Years On, Being Gay Will Be a Non-issue: Wendell Rodricks', *Hill Post Wire*, 19 September 2012, ,https://hillpost.in/2012/09/20-years-on- being-gay-will-be-a-non-issue-wendell-rodricks/51377/.

Anupama Katakam, 'Ace Fashion Designer Wendell Rodricks Was Equally Passionate About the Environment', *Frontline*, 15 February 2020, https://frontline.thehindu. com/dispatches/article30828196.ece.

Vikram Seth

1. Sheela Reddy, 'It Took Me Long to Come to Terms with Myself. Those Were Painful Years,' *Outlook India*,

5 February 2022, https://www.outlookindia.com/magazine/story/it-took-me-long-to-come-to-terms-with-myself-those-were-painful-years/232671.

2. Angela Atkins, *Vikram Seth's Suitable Boy: A Reader's Guide*, A & C Black, 2002.

3. John Gross, 'The Book of the Times', *The New York Times*, 14 April 1986, https://www.nytimes.com/1986/04/14/books/books-of-the-times-073686.html.

4. Jeremy Gavron, 'A Suitable Joy', *The Guardian*, 27 March 1999, https://www.theguardian.com/books/1999/mar/27/books.guardianreview1.

5. Sheela Reddy, 'It Took Me Long to Come to Terms with Myself. Those Were Painful Years', *Outlook India*, 5 February 2022. https://www.outlookindia.com/magazine/story/it-took-me-long-to-come-to-terms-with-myself-those-were-painful-years/232671.

6. Ibid.

7. Amelia Gentleman, 'India's Anti-gay Law Faces Challenge – Asia – Pacific – International Herald Tribune', *The New York Times*, 15 September 2006, https://www.nytimes.com/2006/09/15/world/asia/15iht-india.2827849.html.

8. 'Vikram Seth on Section 377 and Gay Rights in India', *India Today*, 6 September 2018, https://www.indiatoday.in/magazine/cover-story/story/20131230-vikram-seth-on-gay-rights-homosexuality-769369-2013-12-19.

9. Ibid.

10. Soutik Biswas, 'Why Indian Author Vikram Seth is Angry', BBC, 20 December 2013, https://www.bbc.com/news/world-asia-india-25459648.

11. Sandip Roy, 'The Gay Child Needs More Love: Leila Seth on Vikram Seth', Firstpost, 1 February 2012, https://www.firstpost.com/living/the-gay-child-needs-more-love-leila-seth-on-vikram-seth-200154.html.

12. Leila Seth, 'India, You're criminal if Gay', *The New York Times*, 20 March 2014, https://www.nybooks.com/articles/2014/03/20/india-youre-criminal-if-gay/.

13. Rohini Swamy, 'I Only Wish Homosexuals Across India Would Be Able to Come Out: Vikram Seth', *ThePrint*, 11 February 2018, https://theprint.in/theprint-otc/indian-society-opening-sexuality-want-slam-door-shut-vikram-seth/34900/.

14. '"My Gay Son Is Not a Criminal" – Remembering Justice Leila Seth', Homegrown, 8 June 2021, https://homegrown.co.in/homegrown-explore/my-gay-son-is-not-a-criminal-remembering-justice-leila-seth.

Additional Sources

Adam Taylor, 'Read the Beautiful Essay on Love by an Indian Author Whose Sexuality Has Been Outlawed', Business Insider, 20 December 2013, https://www.businessinsider.com/indian-author-vikram-seth-writes-essay-on-love-2013-12?r=US&IR=T.

Jason Burke, 'Vikram Seth: India's Gay Sex Ban Is Against Our Tradition of Tolerance', *The Guardian*, 20 December 2013, https://www.theguardian.com/world/2013/dec/20/vikram-seth-india-supreme-court-ban-gay-sex.

Anmol Arora, 'Vikram Seth Picks up the Mighty Pen to Show His Support', *Man's World India*, 23 March 2022, https://www.mansworldindia.com/currentedition/mw-anniversary-special-vikram-seth-picks-up-the-mighty-pen-in-his-support-of-the-lgbtq-community/.

Chintan Girish Modi, 'Essay: Maan, Firoz and Queer Love in a Suitable Boy', *Hindustan Times*, 7 September 2020, https://www.hindustantimes.com/books/essay-maan-firoz-and-queer-love-in-a-suitable-boy/story-901PuyksROxs86HI7kZCyN.html.

Cydney Yeates, 'A Suitable Boy: Gay Undertone Between Maan Kapoor and Best Friend Confirmed by Producer', *Metro*, 26 July 2020, https://metro.co.uk/2020/07/26/suitable-boy-gay-undertones-confirmed-producer-13039983/.

Ritu Dalmia

1. Ritu Dalmia (As told to Prachi Bhuchar), 'My Freedom to Love: "I Was 23 When I Realised I was Gay. I Told My Parents. The Next Day They Sent a Box of Mangoes for my Partner At the Time"', *India Today*, 22 August 2016, https://www.indiatoday.in/magazine/independence-day-special/story/20160822-ritu-dalmia-my-freedom-to-love-article-377-lgbt-gay-rights-829406-2016-08-12.

2. Ibid.

3. Punita Sabharwal, 'The Diva with a Difference', *Entrepreneur*, 11 November 2018, https://www.entrepreneur.com/en-in/entrepreneurs/i-was-never-ashamed-about-it-chef-ritu-dalmia-on-her/322726.

4. Ibid.

5. Ritu Dalmia (As told to Prachi Bhuchar), 'My Freedom to Love: "I Was 23 When I Realised I was Gay. I Told My

Parents. The Next Day They Sent a Box of Mangoes for my Partner at the Time'", *India Today*, 22 August 2016, https://www.indiatoday.in/magazine/independence-day-special/story/20160822-ritu-dalmia-my-freedom-to-love-article-377-lgbt-gay-rights-829406-2016-08-12.

6.. Ibid.

7. Krishna Priya Pallavi, 'Petitioner Ritu Dalmia on Section 377 Verdict: I Was Trolled. Today I'm Proud', *India Today*, 7 September 2018, https://www.indiatoday.in/lifestyle/people/story/petitioner-ritu-dalmia-on-section-377-verdict-i-was-trolled-but-today-i-m-proud-1333741-2018-09-06.

8. 'Life Doesn't Change if You're Straight or Gay: Ritu Dalmia', *The Indian Express*, 12 July 2018, https://indianexpress.com/article/parenting/family/life-doesnt-change-if-youre-straight-or-gay-ritu-dalmia-5255371/.

Additional Sources

Shivangi Lolayekar, 'GQ Heroes: Ritu Dalmia', *GQ India*, 19 October 2020, https://www.gqindia.com/get-smart/content/gq-heroes-ritu-dalmia.

'Ritu Dalmia', Egomonk Insights, https://insights.egomonk.com/ritu-dalmia-2020/.

Amy Kazim, 'Trailblazers bring Indian Sexuality out of the Shadows', *Financial Times*, 30 May 2018, https://www.ft.com/content/4d9393cc-633f-11e8-90c2-9563a0613e56.

Ritu Dalmia (As told to Sonam Joshi), 'Aren't You the Lesbian Who Filed the Case, the Lawyer Said', *The Times of India*, 7 September 2018, https://timesofindia.indiatimes.com/city/

delhi/arent-you-the-lesbian-who-filed-the-case-a-lawyer-said/articleshow/65714048.cms.

'I Set My Alarm at 5:30 Am in UK to Hear Section 377 Verdict: Ritu Dalmia', *ThePrint*, 6 September 2018, https://theprint.in/opinion/i-set-my-alarm-at-530-am-in-uk-to-hear-section-377-verdict-ritu-dalmia/112923/.

Priyasha Khandelwal, 'Ritu Dalmia, One of the Petitioners Challenging Section 377, on This Fight for Justice', IndianWomenBlog, 7 September 2018, https://www.indianwomenblog.org/ritu-dalmia-one-of-the-petitioners-challenging-section-377-on-this-fight-for-justice/.

'Ritu Dalmia Facts for Kids', Kiddle, https://kids.kiddle.co/Ritu_Dalmia.

Somak Ghoshal and Bibek Bhattacharya, 'Relief and Hope at the End of a Rocky Road', *Mint*, 6 September 2018, https://www.livemint.com/Politics/p9QtN2QFRYVPlbueYBY0YJ/Relief-and-hope-at-the-end-of-a-rocky-road.html.

Sneha Bhura, 'I See Some Hope Now,' *The Week*, 23 September 2018, https://www.theweek.in/theweek/cover/2018/09/14/i-see-some-hope-now.html.

Menaka Guruswamy and Arundhati Katju

1. '377. Unnatural Offences', Indian Kanoon, https://indiankanoon.org/doc/1569253/.

2. 'Lawyers Menaka Guruswamy & Arundhati Katju, the Face of Historic Section 377 Verdict, Reveal They're a Couple', *The Economic Times*, 20 July 2019, https://economictimes.indiatimes.com/magazines/panache/

lawyers-menaka-guruswamy-arundhati-katju-the-face-of-historic-section-377-verdict-reveal-theyre-a-couple/articleshow/70304218.cms.

3. Shivam Vij, 'Why the Legal Challenge to Section 377 Is Much Stronger This Time', *ThePrint*, 16 July 2018, https://theprint.in/opinion/why-the-legal-challenge-to-section-377-is-much-stronger-this-time/83644.

4. Ibid.

5. Ibid.

6. 'Profile With Menaka Guruswamy', The Rhodes Project, https://rhodesproject.com/menaka-guruswamy-profile/.

7. Ibid.

8. Arpan Chaturvedi, 'Who Argued What In Challenge Against Section 377', BQ Prime, 6 September 2018, https://www.bqprime.com/law-and-policy/2018/09/05/who-argued-what-in-challenge-against-section-377.

9. Danish Sheikh, 'Menaka Guruswamy: LGBT Indians Deserve Protection of Their Court, Their Constitution, Their Country', *National Herald*, 12 July 2018, https://www.nationalheraldindia.com/india/advocate-menaka-guruswamy-in-supreme-court-before-constitution-bench-lgbt-indians-deserve-protection-of-their-court-their-constitution-their-country-section-377.

10. Ibid.

11. 'Navtej Singh Johar vs Union of India', Indian Kanoon, 6 September 2018, https://indiankanoon.org/doc/168671544/.

12. 'Karan Johar Leads Bollywood in Hailing Sc's SEC 377 Verdict, Says Country Gets Its Oxygen Back', *Hindustan*

Times, 6 September 2018, https://www.hindustantimes.
com/bollywood/karan-johar-leads-bollywood-in-hailing-
sc-s-sec-377-verdict-says-country-gets-its-oxygen-back/
story-EzQPDG8h2bXpZhYrdei1iL.html.
13. Fareed Zakaria, 'On GPS: Fighting LGBT Discrimination
in India', CNN, 16 July 2019, cnn.com/videos/tv/2019.

Additional Sources

Shivangi Mukherjee, 'Menaka Guruswamy on for Same-
Sex Marriage: "Right to Life of Dignity"', SheThePeople,
18 April 2023, https://www.shethepeople.tv/home-
top-video/menaka-guruswamy-on-same-sex-marriage-
supreme-court/.

Kahini Iyer, 'The Menaka Guruswamy–Arundhati Katju
Romance Is the Love Story We Need in 2019', *Qrius*,
6 September 2018, https://qrius.com/the-menaka-
guruswamy-arundhati-katju-romance-is-the-love-story-
we-need-in-2019/.

Krishnadas Rajagopal, 'The various petitions around same sex
marriage', *The Hindu*, 17 April 2023, https://www.thehindu.
com/news/national/the-various-petitions-around-same-
sex-marriage/article66748868.ece.

Bhadra Sinha, '"Very offensive"– same-sex marriage petitioners
slam Modi govt's "psychology of child" stand in SC',
ThePrint, 13 March 2023, https://theprint.in/judiciary/
very-offensive-same-sex-marriage-petitioners-slam-modi-
govts-psychology-of-child-stand-in-sc/1440591/.

Grace Banu

1. Neville Bhandara, 'Vogue Warriors: Meet Grace Banu, the Transwoman Fighting to Ensure the Safety of India's Trans Folx Through This Pandemic', *Vogue India*, 21 April 2020, https://www.vogue.in/culture-and-living/content/vogue-warriors-grace-banu-tamil-nadu-transwoman-fighting-for-safety-of-indian-trans-folx-covid-19.

2. Akanksha Singh, 'Grace Banu on Visibility, Identity, and Giving Back', *Seema Magazine*, 9 June 2021, https://www.seema.com/grace-banu-on-visibility-identity-and-giving-back.

3. Neville Bhandara, 'Vogue Warriors: Meet Grace Banu, the Transwoman Fighting to Ensure the Safety of India's Trans Folx Through This Pandemic', *Vogue India*, 21 April 2020, https://www.vogue.in/culture-and-living/content/vogue-warriors-grace-banu-tamil-nadu-transwoman-fighting-for-safety-of-indian-trans-folx-covid-19.

4. Kayalvizhi Arivalan, 'A Warrior in Every Way: Dalit and Transgender Activist Grace Banu', *Femina*, 29 September 2021, https://www.femina.in/trending/achievers/a-warrior-in-every-way-dalit-and-transgender-activist-grace-banu-203289.html.

5. Neville Bhandara, 'Vogue Warriors: Meet Grace Banu, the Transwoman Fighting to Ensure the Safety of India's Trans Folx Through This Pandemic', *Vogue India*, 21 April 2020.

6. Meenakshy Sasikumar, 'Explained: Why Trans People Are Demanding Horizontal Reservation Across Castes', The Quint, 15 June 2023, https://www.thequint.com/explainers/trans-people-fight-for-horizontal-reservations-across-castes.

7. Ibid.
8. Tweet from GRACE BANU @thirunangai, 19 April 2023, https://twitter.com/thirunangai/status/1648503101719187458.
9. Akanksha Singh, 'Grace Banu on Visibility, Identity, and Giving Back', *Seema Magazine*, 9 June 2021.

Additional Sources

'Grace Banu', Egomonk Insights, 9 November 2020, https://insights.egomonk.com/grace-banu-2020/.

Ria Mazumdar, 'Grace Banu Fights for Dalit Trans Empowerment', *South Asian Today*, 3 July 2021, https://southasiantoday.com.au/article-9169-grace-banu-fights-for-dalit-trans-empowerment-details.aspx.

Aisiri Amin, 'The Long Fight for Horizontal Reservation for Transgender People', *Mint*, 18 April 2023, https://lifestyle.livemint.com/news/talking-point/the-long-fight-for-horizontal-reservation-for-transgender-people-111681814106470.html.

Runa Mukherjee Parikh, 'You Go Banu! Meet the First Transgender to Ace an Engg Seat in TN', The Quint, https://www.thequint.com/gender/lgbt/you-go-banu-meet-the-first-transgender-to-ace-an-engg-seat-in-tn#read-more.

Korina Estrada, 'Publishing House for Trans Writers Opens in India', Transgenderfeed, 6 March 2023, https://transgenderfeed.com/2023/03/06/publishing-house-for-trans-writers-opens-in-india/.

Dalit Camera, 'Grace Banu – India's first transgender

engineering student, & activist', YouTube, 2 July 2016, https://www.youtube.com/watch?v=1WAVhQQKfTo.

Trans Rights Now Collective, 'Statement Demanding Horizontal Reservation for Transgender Persons', Paalputhu Pakkangali, 5 December 2021, https://www.paalputhumai. com/statement-demanding-horizontal-reservation-for-transgender-persons.

'Grace Banu', Wikipedia, 18 February 2023, https:// en.wikipedia.org/wiki/Grace_Banu.

Madhu Bai Kinnar

1. Shaikh Azizur Rahman, 'India's First Openly Transgender Mayor Takes Office, Fueling Hope for Rights', VOA, 9 January 2015, https://www.voanews.com/a/hopeful-signs-for-rights-as-indias-first-openly-transgender-mayor-takes-office/2591652.html.

2. Eesha Patkar, 'India's Transgender Mayor – Is the Country Finally Overcoming Prejudice?' *The Guardian*, 3 March 2015, https://www.theguardian.com/cities/2015/mar/03/india-first-transgender-mayor-overcoming-prejudice-hijra.

3. Agence France-Presse, 'Transgender Woman is Elected District Mayor in Indian State of Chhattisgarh', *The Guardian*, 5 January 2015, https://www.theguardian.com/world/2015/jan/05/transgender-woman-elected-mayor-india-chhattisgarh.

4. Eesha Patkar, 'India's Transgender Mayor – Is the Country Finally Overcoming Prejudice?' *The Guardian*, 03 March 2015.

5. Ibid.

Rituparno Ghosh

1. Palash Ghosh, 'Renowned Indian Filmmaker And Gay Icon Rituparno Ghosh Dies at 49', *IBT*, 30 May 2013, https://www.ibtimes.com/renowned-indian-filmmaker-gay-icon-rituparno-ghosh-dies-49-1284615.

2. Subhash K. Jha, 'Rituparno Ghosh, a man paranoid about his own sexuality', *India Today*, 31 May 2013, https://www.indiatoday.in/movies/celebrities/story/rituparno-ghosh-paranoid-sexuality-165062-2013-05-30.

3. Nisharga Pratim Bhattacharjee, 'Gender Through the Lens of Rituparno Ghosh', LinkedIn, 25 July 2022, https://www.linkedin.com/pulse/gender-through-lens-rituparno-ghosh-nisharga-pratim-bhattacharjee-/.

4. 'Remembering Rituparno: When the Master Filmmaker Talked to Tellychakkar About Homosexuality in Films', TellyChakkar, 06 March 2013, https://www.tellychakkar.com/movie/interview/remembering-rituparno-when-the-master-filmmaker-talked-tellychakkar-about.

5. Tweet from Anupam Kher [@AnupamPKher]30 May 2013, https://twitter.com/anupampkher/status/339984859357388800.

6. Tweet from Amitabh Bachchan [@SrBachchan], 31 May 2013, https://twitter.com/SrBachchan/status/340193175283044353?lang=en.

7. Tweet from Amitabh Bachchan [@SrBachchan], 31 May 2013, https://twitter.com/SrBachchan/status/340193448697159680.

8. 'Mamata Visits Rituparno Ghosh's Home, Calls His Death a Sad Day for Bengal', *The Times of India*, 30 May 2013,

https://timesofindia.indiatimes.com/india/mamata-visits-rituparno-ghoshs-home-calls-his-death-a-sad-day-for-bengal/articleshow/20345845.cms.

9. Snigdha Banerjee, 'Rituparno Ghosh: Queer, Art and Expression', CitySpidey, 4 June 2021, https://www.cityspidey.com/news/13845/rituparno-ghosh-queer-art-and-expression.

Additional Sources

'Rituparno Ghosh: Indian Film Director Dies Age 49', *The Guardian*, 30 May 2013, https://www.theguardian.com/film/2013/may/30/rituparno-ghosh-indian-film-director-dies.

Raja Sen, 'Rituparno, Tender as Night: Raja Sen Salutes the Talent', Rediff.com, 30 May 2013, https://www.rediff.com/movies/column/rituparno-tender-as-night-raja-sen-salutes-the-talent/20130530.htm.

'Rituparno Ghosh, Trailblazer of New Wave Bengali Cinema, Dies', *The Times of India*, 30 May 2013, https://timesofindia.indiatimes.com/entertainment/hindi/bollywood/news/rituparno-ghosh-trailblazer-of-new-wave-bengali-cinema-dies/articleshow/20346594.cms.

Bharati Dubey, 'Amitabh Bachchan tweets in memory of Rituparno Ghosh', Indiatimes, 31 May 2013, https://timesofindia.indiatimes.com/entertainment/hindi/bollywood/news/amitabh-bachchan-tweets-in-memory-of-rituparno-ghosh/articleshow/20358093.cms.

Nisharga Pratim Bhattacharjee, 'Gender Through the Lens

of Rituparna Ghosh', Linkedin, 25 July 2022, https://www.linkedin.com/pulse/gender-through-lens-rituparno-ghosh-nisharga-pratim-bhattacharjee-/.

Subhash K. Jha, Revisiting Rituparna Ghosh's Memories in March, *The Times of India*, 2 April 2023, https://timesofindia.indiatimes.com/entertainment/hindi/bollywood/news/revisting-rituparno-ghoshs-memories-in-march/articleshow/99176904.cms.

'Indian Media: Tributes Pour in for Rituparno Ghosh', BBC, 31 May 2013, https://www.bbc.co.uk/news/world-asia-india-22726455.

Subhash K. Jha, 'Rituparno Ghosh, You Are Much Missed', Firstpost, 1 September 2022, https://www.firstpost.com/entertainment/rituparno-ghosh-you-are-much-missed-11157241.html.

'Rituparno Ghosh's Heartwarming Connection With the Bachchan', *The Times of India*, 31 August 2022, https://timesofindia.indiatimes.com/entertainment/bengali/movies/news/rituparno-ghoshs-heartwarming-connection-with-the-bachchan-family/articleshow/93907567.cms.

Sumana Mukherjee, 'Rituparno Ghosh Braved to Script the Story of His Own Transgender World', Cityspidey, 31 March 2023, https://www.cityspidey.com/news/20750/rituparno-ghosh-braved-to-script-the-story-of-his-own-transgender-world.

'Rituparno Ghosh: Bengali Filmmaker Dies in India', BBC, 30 May 2013, https://www.bbc.co.uk/news/world-asia-india-22712973.

Shanku Sharma, 'Rituparno Ghosh – Renaissance Man of New Wave Bengali Cinema', FilmSpell, 21 August 2020, https://filmspell.com/rituparno-ghosh-renaissance-man-of-new-wave-bengali-cinema/.

Vidushi Trivedi, 'Rituparno Ghosh and His Art of Sensitive Storytelling', Culture Trip, 30 December 2016, https://theculturetrip.com/asia/india/articles/rituparno-ghosh-and-his-art-of-sensitive-storytelling/

Nermeen Shaikh, 'Rituparno Ghosh and the 'Intellectual Film' in India', Asia Society, https://asiasociety.org/rituparno-ghosh-and-intellectual-film-india.

Yashika Jethwani, 'Rituparno Ghosh / Queer Figure of Indian Cinema', Failure Before Success, 17 May 2022, https://failurebeforesuccess.com/rituparno-ghosh/.

Ruchira Talapatra, 'The Queer Lens of Rituparno Ghosh', *Deccan Herald*, 29 January 2016, https://www.deccanherald.com/content/525675/queer-lens-rituparno-ghosh.html.

Yajnaseni Chakraborty, 'Rituparno Ghosh Was Extremely Lonely', Rediff.com, 30 May 2013, https://m.rediff.com/movies/column/rituparno-ghosh-was-extremely-lonely/20130530.htm.

Dutee Chand

1. 'The "rebirth" of Indian sprinter Dutee Chand', BBC News, 29 July 2015, https://www.bbc.com/news/world-asia-india-33699201.

2. Amrit Dhillon, '"No One Can Live Wthout Love": Athlete Dutee Chand, India's LGBT Trailblazer', *The Guardian*, 10 June 2019, https://www.theguardian.com/world/2019/

jun/10/no-one-can-live-without-love-athlete-dutee-chand-indias-lgbt-trailblazer.

3. 'The "rebirth" of Indian sprinter Dutee Chand', BBC News, 29 July 2015.

4. Ibid.

5. Ibid.

6. Ibid.

7. 'Coming Out of Closet Is Better Than Hiding My Relationship: Dutee Chand', *The Times of India*/PTI, 25 August 2019, https://timesofindia.indiatimes.com/sports/more-sports/athletics/coming-out-of-closet-is-better-than-hiding-my-relationship-dutee-chand/articleshow/70827804.cms.

8 'Dutee Chand: India's First Openly Gay Athlete', Aljazeera, 20 May 2019, https://www.aljazeera.com/sports/2019/5/20/dutee-chand-indias-first-openly-gay-athlete.

9 'Ellen Degeneres Proud of India's Dutee Chand for Coming Out, Says "She Knows a Thing or Two About Being First"', *Hindustan Times*, 22 may 2019, https://www.hindustantimes.com/tv/ellen-degeneres-proud-of-india-s-dutee-chand-for-coming-out-says-she-knows-a-thing-or-two-about-being-first/story-8vLqMvEHdaTMka4PrUTU4J.html.

10. Sheree Gomes Gupta, 'Dutee Chand on the Backlash She Faced After Coming Out: "I Was Made to Feel Like I Did Not Deserve to Live"', *Vogue India*, 05 November 2019, https://www.vogue.in/culture-and-living/content/dutee-chand-vogue-india-interview-backlash-after-coming-out-as-lesbian-lgbtqi.

11. Amrit Dhillon, '"No One Can Live Wthout Love": Athlete Dutee Chand, India's LGBT Trailblazer', *The Guardian*, 10 June 2019, https://www.theguardian.com/world/2019/jun/10/no-one-can-live-without-love-athlete-dutee-chand-indias-lgbt-trailblazer.
12. Ibid.
13. '"I Feel Everyone Should Get This Right": Dutee Chand on Same-Sex Marriage', ESPN, 12 May 2023, https://www.espn.in/athletics/story/_/id/37612269/i-feel-everyone-get-right-dutee-chand-same-sex-marriage-supreme-court.

Additional Sources

'India's First Openly Gay Sprinter Dutee Chand Posts Photo With Girlfriend, Sparks Marriage Rumours', *India Today*, 2 December 2022, https://www.indiatoday.in/sports/other-sports/story/dutee-chand-announces-marriage-with-girlfriend-2304590-2022-12-02.

'"I Keep Alive Your Power in My Heart": Dutee Chand Shares Image With Her Partner on Savitri Brat', *The Indian Express*, 19 May 2023, https://indianexpress.com/article/sports/sport-others/i-keep-alive-your-power-in-er-partner-on-savitri-brat-8618915/.

Manjiri Chitre, 'Dutee Chand Opens Up on Same-Sex Marriage: "...They Don't Speak Out Due to Fear"', *Hindustan Times*, 12 May 2023, https://www.hindustantimes.com/india-news/dutee-chand-opens-up-on-same-sex-marriage-they-dont-speak-out-due-to-fear-101683902487724.html.

Reshma

1. Hirra Azmat, 'Reshma: The Story of Resilience', *The Kashmir Monitor*, 6 November 2022, https://www.thekashmirmonitor.net/reshma-the-story-of-resilience/.
2. Ibid.
3. Khalid Bashir Gura, 'Reshma is Dead, Why (S)he Was a Very Important Person?', *Kashmir Life*, 6 November 2022, https://kashmirlife.net/reshma-is-dead-why-she-was-a-very-important-person-303606/.
4. Ibid.
5. Zoya Mateen and Moazum Mohammad, 'Reshma: The Kashmir Trans Icon Who Fought Pain to Bring Joy to People', BBC News, 17 November 2022, https://www.bbc.com/news/world-asia-india-63539236.
6. Shefali Rafiq, 'A Glimpse into the Lives of Transgender People in Kashmir', openDemocracy, 21 December 2021, https://www.opendemocracy.net/en/5050/transgender-people-in-kashmir/.
7. Khalid Bashir Gura, 'Reshma is Dead, Why (S)he Was a Very Important Person?', *Kashmir Life*, 06 November 2022, https://kashmirlife.net/reshma-is-dead-why-she-was-a-very-important-person-303606/.
8. 'Life and Legacy of Reshma: Kashmir's Most Influential Transgender Figure', *Kashmir Walla*, 07 November 2022, https://thekashmirwalla.com/life-and-legacy-of-reshma-kashmirs-most-influential-transgender-figure/.

9. Aakriti Handa, 'Remembering Reshma: The Voice of Transgender People in Kashmir', The Quint, 29 November 2022, https://www.thequint.com/gender/kashmir-reshma-abdul-rashid-transgender-singer-dead-viral-song.

Additional Sources

Saqib Mugloo, 'Kashmir Remembers a Trans Icon', *Himal*, 23 February 2023, https://www.himalmag.com/kashmir-remembers-reshma-transgender-singer-icon/.

Dinesh Manhotra, 'Who Was Singer Abdul Rashid; "Reshma of Kashmir" Singer Passes Away [Details]', *IBT*, 6 November 2022, https://www.ibtimes.co.in/who-was-singer-abdul-rashid-reshma-kashmiri-singer-passes-away-details-853849.

Acknowledgements

I wouldn't be here without my family: Mummy, Papa and Sweety – who fought the world for me.

I want to thank my publisher, Chiki Sarkar, for her brilliance, my agent Kanishka Gupta, who took me under his wings, and Sharif Rangnekar, who, over the years, has supported me in different capacities.

To my dearest friends, who held me in their arms when it was needed the most – Rajindra Vikram Sharma, Rahul Sarkar, Chittajit Mitra and Aman Punia, this book wouldn't have come to life without you.

I want to thank all the media outlets, editors, journalists and people from the literary space who have helped me at every stage.

I dedicate this book to those numerous kothis and hijras in small towns who have shaped my life for all these years – I am grateful for your light.

A Note on the Author

Aditya Tiwari is a poet from Jabalpur. His first book of poems, *April is Lush* (2019), received international acclaim. He holds a postgraduate in Journalism from the University of East Anglia. His work has appeared in *The Telegraph*, *PinkNews*, BBC, *Vice*, *The Times of India*, *Hindustan Times* and elsewhere. He has been featured in *The Washington Post*, *GQ*, *Grazia*, *Vogue*, *Cosmopolitan* and *Elle*, among other places. This is his second book. Learn more about Aditya on Instagram and Twitter at @aprilislush.